Lives of the Laureates

Lives of the Laureates
Seven Nobel Economists

edited by William Breit and Roger W. Spencer

The MIT Press
Cambridge, Massachusetts
London, England

This book was set in Baskerville by The MIT Press Computergraphics Department and printed and bound by Halliday Lithograph in the United States of America.

Library of Congress Cataloging-in-Publication Data

Lives of the laureates.

Bibliography: p.
1. Economists—Biography. 2. Nobel prizes—Biography. I. Breit, William. II. Spencer, Roger W.
HB76.L58 1986   330'.092'2 [B]   86-2919
ISBN 0-262-02255-9

61,840

Contents

Acknowledgments

As scarcely needs saying, an enterprise of this kind requires the cooperation of many people. My thanks, first and foremost, to Ronald Calgaard, president of Trinity University, who not only provided generous funding but threw in a large measure of encouragement from the moment the idea for the lecture series was broached. The dinners given by Ronald and Genie Calgaard in their charming home on the edge of the Trinity University campus were perfect prologues to each Nobel economist's public lecture.

Colleagues in the Department of Economics were unstinting in their enthusiasm. Special mention should be made of Joe Ashby, Richard Butler, Joe Davis, Pedro Fraile, and John Huston, who provided logistical support when needed. David Zorn, a graduate of Trinity University, was of enormous help in checking on the lighting and sound systems prior to each lecture and in providing yeoman's service generally. My secretary, Rita Miller, took care of a myriad of small details and never lost her composure or good cheer.

Finally, thanks are due to the Nobel economists themselves, who not only accepted the challenge of trying to make their chief contributions intelligible to a lay audience but did so in the demanding context of an autobiographical format. Their insights deepened my perspectives and broadened my understanding of the relationship between autobiography and creativity. For that, and for their kind patience and cooperation at all stages of the project, I am grateful.

William Breit

Introduction

This book consists of autobiographical accounts of the careers of seven people who have three qualities in common. First, they are all economists. Second, each of them has been awarded the Alfred Nobel Memorial Prize in Economic Science. Third, each traveled to San Antonio, Texas, to deliver his story in person at Trinity University.

The Nobel Prize in Economics was not created by Alfred Nobel himself. In 1901 his will established prizes in physics, chemistry, medicine or physiology, literature, and peace. He wished to reward specific achievements rather than outstanding persons. In the case of the natural sciences, the awards were to be given for "discoveries," "inventions," and "improvements." In 1968 the Central Bank of Sweden, in connection with its tercentenary celebration, initiated a new award, the Central Bank of Sweden Prize in Economic Science in Memory of Alfred Nobel. This prize was to be granted in conformity with the standards that governed the awarding of the original Nobel prizes. According to the rules established by the Central Bank of Sweden, the "Prize shall be awarded annually to a person who has carried out a work in economic science of the eminent significance expressed in the Will of Alfred Nobel."[1]

The idea for a series of autobiographical lectures by Nobel laureates in economics was that of the senior editor, who has spent a good part of his academic career studying, teaching, and writing about the lives and ideas of leading contemporary American economists. This abiding interest in the relationship between biography and the creative process led naturally to the thought of providing a forum in which outstanding economists would express in their own words, in any way that seemed congenial, a personal memoir under the general rubric, "My Evolution as an Economist." At the very least such a forum would preserve part of the rich record of accomplishment that helped to shape the direction and character of economic science in the post–World War II era. But the larger purpose was to provide important source material for a theory of scientific discovery.

Little is known about the process by which original ideas are germinated and eventually accepted by one's peers. To what extent is the substance of scientific work in social science a reflection of the lives of those who produced it? What is the role of influential teachers and colleagues? To what extent are the problems to which these thinkers addressed themselves a result of their own backgrounds and the economic and social problems of their times? What forces were most responsible for leading them to their insights? In short, what is it that enables an individual to discover something that seizes and holds the attention of a large segment of a scientific community? To help answer such questions was the major rationale behind the lecture series.

But whom to invite? It was clear that budgetary and time constraints would limit the number of invitations, and so the roster was restricted in the following way: (1) only economists who served on the faculties of American universities at the time the Nobel Prize was awarded would be included; and (2) the roster would represent as many different facets of economics in terms of types of contributions, specific areas, methods of analysis, and ideological differences as possible. In 1983, when the program was being planned, there were twelve winners of the Nobel Prize who met the first criterion, although one was too ill to travel. A difficult winnowing process in accordance with the second criterion narrowed the final list to eight. To our pleasant surprise, only one invitee declined to participate.

For most of the participants, the assignment was a difficult one. There is an understandable reluctance to give a public talk about one's own intellectual contributions. As one of the invitees put it, "I do not know that I could keep it between the Scylla of false modesty and the Charybdis of boastfulness, and I am afraid I would find the whole business rather stressful." Moreover, most of their work in its professional formulation was technical in nature, closed off to those not trained as economists. Yet each was being asked to make his contribution accessible to a lay audience at a public lecture open to the whole community. This would provide greater difficulties for some than for others. Samuelson's and Arrow's scientific contributions are largely in the domain of mathematical economics. Klein, Friedman, Stigler, and Tobin make liberal use of statistical techniques and econometrics. All express themselves in the technical vocabulary of their discipline.

And yet in each instance, as the reader of these pages will discover, each speaker somehow managed to convey the nature and significance of his contributions. (The essays in this book are in the order in which they were presented in the Trinity lecture series.) It is hard to imagine a less painful way of grasping the essentials of Kenneth Arrow's "impossibility theorem" than hearing it (or reading about it) in his own words. And is there anywhere a more clearly presented conception of what goes into econometric "model building" than is to be found in Lawrence Klein's essay? George Stigler's masterful explanation of his "information theory" is made luminously clear and understandable to almost everyone with an interest in this fruitful innovation. Indeed, each participant achieved the goal of clarity without sacrificing inherently difficult content.

The visit of each of the Nobel laureates was an unqualified success. The audiences were large and appreciative. Some traveled considerable distances to attend. Each economist met with students and faculty informally. At small receptions, at restaurants, over coffee cups in the faculty lounge, and at dinners in private homes, students and faculty were able to talk with some of the most highly regarded economists of the twentieth century. Notwithstanding their formidable reputations as scholars and, in some instances, as strong personalities, their lack of arrogance impressed almost everyone who came into contact with them. An important side benefit of the lecture series was the lesson that some of the most illustrious figures of modern economics are human after all.

Looking back over these lectures, one is struck by the many currents within the stream of modern economics. The reader will find that paths cross in unexpected ways; that disparate thinkers were often influenced by the same teachers; that luck as well as perseverance and hard work play a role in the successful creation of scientific knowledge. Equally important, these autobiographical essays reveal psychological truths, perhaps hidden from the subjects themselves, which an especially perceptive reader will discern. Taken as a whole, they provide a comprehensive picture of the diverseness, richness, and profundity that is the hallmark of contemporary economic thought in America.

Lives of the Laureates

W. Arthur Lewis

I had never meant to be an economist. My father had wanted me to be a lawyer, but as he died when I was seven he had no vote at the appropriate time. That came when I was awarded the St. Lucia government scholarship in 1932, tenable at any British university. I did not want to be a doctor either; nor a teacher. That put me into a hole, since law, medicine, preaching, and teaching were the only professions open to young blacks in my day. I wanted to be an engineer, but neither the colonial government nor the sugar plantations would hire a black engineer. What to do? My mother, without whom I could not have gone so far, would support whatever I might choose. As I leafed through the University of London prospectus, my eye was caught by something called the Bachelor of Commerce degree, which offered accounting, statistics, business law, business management, economics, a foreign language, and economic history. What was this economics? I had never heard of it before, and nobody in St. Lucia knew what it was—though my sample was small and unrepresentative. No matter. The rest of the degree was very practical and would give me a basis for a job in business or some kind of administrative work. So I settled for this and went off to London for the B.Com. degree in 1933, at the age of eighteen.

At the London School of Economics it turned out that I was good at economics, so when I graduated with a first in 1937 I was given an LSE scholarship to do a Ph.D. in economics. Next year I was appointed for one year as a teaching assistant and the year after that became an assistant lecturer. Years of wondering how I would ever earn a living, and of smiling confidently when friends and relatives pushed the question at me, could now be forgotten. I was going to be an economist.

Though ignorant of economics, I knew what was meant by administration. I had left school in 1929 and had been a junior clerk in the government service for the intervening four years. There I had acquired the clerical skills—to type, make notes, write letters, and file—that helped me as an undergraduate. I became familiar as well with administrative and legal structures, knowledge that would also help me.

Also, of course, I earned some money (three pounds a month) to contribute to the family budget. My mother was unsurpassed in the ways of stretching income, and this, combined with loving care, was what enabled her to bring up five sons, who were all minors when she was widowed. (I was the fourth son.) My mother's story is standard in the life history of achievers. A widow with young children, very little money, an immigrant (my father and she were immigrants from Antigua), the highest integrity, unshakable courage, unlimited faith in God. As a youngster in school, I would hear other boys talking about the superiority of men over women; I used to think that they must be crazy.

I had left school because I had completed the curriculum at the level of the Cambridge School Certificate, which is equivalent to SAT. I had completed at fourteen because when I was six I had had some kind of infection that kept me out of school for three months. My father, a former teacher but at this stage a customs official, said to me, "Don't worry; I will teach you a little every day, so you will not fall behind." This was an understatement. Any intelligent child receiving personal tutoring every day will learn in three months as much as the schoolteacher's class learns in two years. When I returned to school, I was moved up two grades and was still ahead of what was being taught. This was a traumatic experience. It meant that for the rest of my school life I was always in the company of boys two or three years older than myself. They flexed their muscles, but I had nothing to show. They played cricket in the first eleven, whereas I was in the fourth eleven. I acquired an acute inferiority complex with regard to my physique. I learned that acceptance into the group is not a matter of academic performance only: you must meet their criteria as well as your own. I matured faster than I would have done had I stayed in school. I went to England apprehensive that the English eighteen-year-olds would be much better able to handle themselves than I was, only to find that they were not.

Fate had decided that I was to be an economist. What kind of economist I was to be was also settled: an applied economist. This did not mean just that I should apply economics to industrial or other structural problems. It meant that I would approach a problem from its institutional background, recognizing that the solution was as likely to be in the institutional setting as in the economic analysis.

What part of applied economics I would work in was also settled for me, since my assistant lectureship was in the commerce department, under Professor Sir Arnold Plant. He was my mentor, and without his word at crucial points I would have received neither the scholarship nor the assistant lectureship. (This was the school's first black appointment, and there was a little resistance.) He and I had intellectual difficulties, since he was a laissez-faire economist and I was not; but this did not stand in the way of our relationship.

Because Plant was a specialist in the organization of British industry, he put me to lecture in this field and suggested a Ph.D. thesis topic in the field; and so I became an "expert" on

British industrial organization. I liked the subject, so it was no hardship to me.

LSE in the 1930s was (as at any other time) a very lively place. Every point of view was represented on the faculty, and as two or three competing courses of lectures were offered on each "hot" topic, those who understood what was going on had marvellous intellectual feasts. The typical high-achieving LSE student was bright, from the effort to keep up with so many conflicting themes, and skeptical, from learning to distinguish so continually between plausibility and truth. We were reputed to make excellent managers but poor parliamentarians.

The school had not quite caught up with Keynesianism, which was taught by the young lecturers but denounced by the big names. On the other hand, the school was in the forefront of the development and worldwide expansion of neoclassical economics, especially with John Hicks, Roy Allen, Nicholas Kaldor, Friedrich Hayek, and Lionel Robbins.

This was where what I was doing fitted in. Most of the writing in this area was concerned with elaborating the theory: turning words into diagrams and diagrams into equations. I was one of a minority engaged in testing the theories against the facts.

I worked in industrial organization from 1937, when I was given a scholarship for the purpose, until 1948, when I went to Manchester and published *Overhead Costs*, which was essentially an updated version of my Ph.D. thesis.

My interest in overhead costs was the structure of prices in situations where average cost per unit exceeds marginal cost. The Pareto rule was that price should equal marginal cost, but to apply this rule would bankrupt the firm. In practice, such situations oscillate between bankruptcy and monopoly, as in the airline industry today. The general inclination of economists in those cases was to enforce marginal pricing and subsidize firms to the extent of the differences between marginal and average cost. This was hardly practical, as an industry-wide policy. Neither could it be justified, as many taxpayers would be forced to pay for services that they did not use. If one started from the premise that those who use the service should pay for it, the problem reduced to how to spread the fixed costs among the users. Here I started from the railway principle of "charging what the traffic will bear" and linked up with the new price discrimination theory, as elaborated by Joan Robinson.

Another aspect of overhead costs was the time dimension. Demand was not steady, but fluctuated. If the output could not be stored, there would be times of idle capacity, regular or irregular; how was the cost of this to be shared? I demonstrated that the correct approach to this problem was to treat the fixed investment as a producer in joint cost of different outputs at different times, each paying what it could bear, and subject to the sum of payments not exceeding total cost.

The main point of my thesis was, therefore, to examine in the light of these approaches to overhead costs those price systems found in industry other than the simple unit price per unit of output. These included two-part tariffs, time of day pricing, quantity discounts, loyalty discounts, and such related systems as trading stamps and tied purchases. My interest also overlapped into the history of the laws relating to pricing. With the spread of price regulation in Britain over the next twenty years my book had a ready-made audience.

This analysis of industrial structure was the background to what I was writing in my spare time, so to speak, which included a small book called the *Principles of Economic Planning*, published in 1949. The Fabian Society is one hundred years old this year. It is the thinking arm of the British Labour Party, though in fact it is older than the Labour Party and quite independent of it. I went to one of its conferences in 1947 and was roundly abused for a paper I read on the importance of avoiding inflation and on the measures required for that outcome. I in my turn was horrified by the sentiments of the members on this subject, and said to the secretary: "You really ought to commission a study on the problems and pitfalls of administering a mixed economy." "Why don't you do it," he said, and after thinking about the subject for a little time I agreed to do so.

Fabian pamphlets usually run from twenty to thirty pages, but his one came out at more than one hundred pages, not because of my long-windedness but because it takes at least that to discuss in detail how to run a mixed economy. The book was not original, but it was timely. It addressed itself exclusively to the problems of Great Britain in the year 1948, but nonetheless was translated into several languages and sold widely all over the world. Its prescriptions for evading inflation were Keynesian and turned on the feasibility of keeping money incomes rising at not more than 3 percent a year. On rereading the book recently for this occasion, the only other point that catches my eye is that governments of mixed economies, coming into power on a wave of popular frustration, always run straight onto the rocks of the balance of payments and have to reverse themselves (for example, France in 1936 and 1981; Britain in 1945; Jamaica in 1976). Somebody should write a manual called something like "The First Two Years," which would map the problems by which the mixed economy is assailed as a new social democratic government moves to implement its program. But that will have to be some other author.

Let me come back to my academic program. I gather that the sponsors of this set of lectures hope to see how one's thinking is tied to one's environment. I am not a very good example. I began by showing you that I became an economist when I really wanted to be an engineer, bcame a university teacher because there was nothing else for me to do, and became an applied economist because that was my mentor's subject. The next phase of this story continues in the same vein. I am not complaining; fate has been kinder to me than to most other persons. I am merely recording what happened.

I dropped industrial economics in 1945 to teach another subject not of my own choosing, namely a survey of the world economy between the two wars. This came about in the following way. The acting chairman of the economics department in 1945 was Friedrich Hayek. One day he said to me, "We fill up our students with trade cycle theory and explanations of the great depression, but the entering class was born in 1927, cannot remember the depression, and has no idea what we are talking about. Why don't you give a course of lectures on what happened between the wars?" "The answer to your question," I said, "is very easy. It is that I myself have no idea what happened between the wars." "Well," said Hayek, "the best way to learn a subject is to teach it." So that was how I came some four years later to publish a small book entitled *Economic Survey 1919–1939*, summarizing what we then thought we knew about the world economy between 1919 and 1939.

Nowadays we would see this as a job for an econometrician, but econometrics had not yet established the despotism over economics that it wields today. Tinbergen had pointed the way, with his model of the British economy before the wars, but indicated only the general direction. Also, the figures for the 1920s were sparse and those for the 1930s only slightly less so. I had hoped to get cues by reading the economics literature of the time, especially the financial weeklies, but they yielded next to nothing. We use language differently today. Economists pepper their sentences with percentages and billions, even in the daily newspaper, and even the lay reader is expected to keep a personal computer in his head that enables him to jump from one measurement to another. Prewar economists spoke of "many" or "a few" or "some" and avoided figures.

Looking back, I feel that I was more successful in treating the great depression of the 1930s than the alleged prosperity of the 1920s. The Americans persuaded themselves that the American economy was more prosperous than ever before in the second half of the 1920s, but this is not borne out by the statistics, which reveal only average performance. Dazzled by this misconception, one tended to see prosperity all over the world in the 1920s and to underrate the comparative stagnation of world trade and the effects of that stagnation. Staple industrial products were in surplus supply, especially textiles, steel, ships, and coal, creating for Britain, Germany, Japan, and India pools of unemployment in industrial centers. The economists of the day saw the troubles mostly in terms of inappropriate exchange rates; we would call this structural unemployment and seek more activist remedies. My book neither asked nor answered why the ten years following the end of World War I would lead into a great depression while the ten years following World War II would lead to unprecedented prosperity. Part of the answer has to be that the world economy was more unstable in the second half of the 1920s than it was in the first half of the 1950s.

Paradoxically, the great depression of the 1930s was easier to untangle. The first question to be avoided was, What caused the depression? Our large bundle of trade cycle theories offered a wide range of possible causes, each of which was sufficient, though it might not be necessary. One might as well fight an octopus as proceed along these lines.

My approach was to accept that industrial recessions had occurred from time to time over the preceding century with intervals of four to ten years, and that the problem was not why there was a recession in 1929, but why, having started, it had become so deep. What distinguished the outbreak of this particular sequence? One cannot give an account of the great depression in two paragraphs, but one can list the decisive elements. These are seven.

1. In the U.S. economy prosperity coincided with a railway-construction-immigration-housing cycle. Congress having restricted immigration from 1924, the construction boom of the

second half of the 1920s was weak, and the abnormal weakness of the first half of the thirties weakened the whole economy.

2. Both domestic and international agricultural prices had been falling since the mid-1920s, capacity having grown faster than demand. Rural consumption was low, and in the U.S. an abnormal number of rural banks failed.

3. Monetary and fiscal authorities believed that the best way to revive production was to reduce the flow of income and acted accordingly. This action presumably worsened the depression.

4. The industrial slump was as bad in Germany as in the U.S. The weakness of the one compounded the weakness of the other.

5. Capitalists everywhere lost confidence and reduced their investment flows. This spiraled. Less investment meant less production, less income, more excess capacity, less investment, and so on.

6. The New York Stock Exchange, which had talked itself into overconfidence in the late twenties, now talked itself down and reflected all the unpleasantness occurring elsewhere.

7. One country after another left the gold standard, imposed exchange controls, and raised tariff levels. International trade fell by 30 percent in volume.

Such a list as this does not show the relative magnitude of these elements, their sequences, or their interrelationships: that is the econometrician's job. It serves only my immediate purpose, which was to show that it was not strange that there was a great depression in 1929, since so many weaknesses came together at that point.

Publication of the book still left two questions unanswered in my mind, on which I would spend a good part of my academic life. The first of these is what determines the terms of trade between industrial and primary products. This question was central to the book, in that the weakness of agricultural prices communicated itself throughout the economy increasingly after 1925, bankrupting farmers, bringing down banks, and forcing countries off the gold standard. But the question was also central to my life, since my home country was subject to violent swings in agricultural prices that played havoc with attempts to manage the economy with some stability.

My subsequent work on the terms of trade started from the observation that there was a constant relationship between an index of world industrial production and an index of world trade in primary products. This relationship said that a 1 percent rise in industrial production was associated with about 0.87 percent rise in world trade in primary products. This relationship extended all the way back to 1873 and all the way forward to 1973, though it did not hold before 1873. In the process I made and published indexes of world industrial production, world trade in manufactures and in primary products, and prices of tropical products and of manufactures back to 1870, in some cases to 1850.

On the theoretical side the short-run determinants of the terms of trade must be demand and supply. One could model and calculate the short-run elasticities for various groups of commodities. The long-run terms for tropical crops, I have suggested (in the model that I will reach in a moment), are determined by the infinite elasticity of supply of tropical produce, and therefore are not affected by changes in demand. Infinite elasticity springs from the fact that agricultural exports are a small part of tropical agriculture output—under 20 percent—and can in the long run (say, over twenty years) be expanded or contracted at constant cost. That cost is very small, since the yield in food cultivation is very small. This analysis has momentous consequences, for it means that the farmers would do better to grow more food than to put resources into more export crops. This controversy is still heated.

Now I come to the second question left over from my book on 1919–1939. As soon as one started to work on the great depression, one was faced by the question whether this was a unique event that had never happened before or whether this was merely one of a series. I worked on this subject off and on from 1950 until publishing my book *Growth and Fluctuations 1870–1913* in 1978. This long period results from my nine years of absence from university study and partly from the labor performed in collecting and preparing materials, including the indexes mentioned a moment ago.

To the question of whether the great depression was unique, the answer was yes and no. No: the United States had a major recession about once every twenty years. Yes: the great depression of 1929 was much greater than any of its predecessors.

The dates of the major recessions were 1872, 1892, 1906, and 1929. (The series, incidentally, continues at 1956 and 1973.) They are called Kuznets depressions because the sequence was first identified by Simon Kuznets. We know a great deal about them, thanks to the work of Abramovitz. They resulted from a long construction cycle, in which, starting from the bottom, frenzied railway building would be resumed, followed by immigration, followed by residential construction. The economy would have about ten years of prosperity followed by ten years incorporating the Kuznets recession. The continuation of this series after World War II, in 1956 and 1973, was unexpected because railway construction had ended and immigration was greatly restricted and noncyclical. Presumably, in the U.S. as in other countries residential building is big enough to impose a twenty-year cycle on the whole economy.

So much for the twenty-year cycle. It was also alleged that there was a fifty-year cycle, where twenty-five years of relative prosperity would be followed by twenty-five years of relative stagnation. This one was named after Kondratieff, the Russian economist who invented the idea. I worked very hard on this one for my book *Growth and Fluctuations* and did not find evidence of a fifty-year cycle in world industrial production. Agriculture had a turning point in 1899. Agricultural output grew faster from 1873 to 1899 than it did from 1899 to 1920. Agricultural prices rose after 1899, having previously been falling. Real wages slowed down after 1899 because of rising prices. Exports of manufactures grew faster after 1899 partly because of the altered terms of trade. It is not disputed that agricultural output and prices show this change of trend after 1899; but the decisive question is whether world *industrial* production grew faster after 1899, and the answer seems to be no. The long recession that we have had since 1973 has revived Kondratieff, and his literature is growing fast in Europe. This controversy too is heating up.

Let me come back to autobiography. My research career falls into three parts. First I studied industrial structure. Second I tackled the history of the world economy, from the middle of the nineteenth century. And third I worked on problems of economic development. I have told you about the first two and now come to economic development.

My interest in the subject was an offshoot of my anti-imperialism. I can remember my father taking me to a meeting of the local Marcus Garvey association when I was seven years old. So it is not surprising that the first thing I ever published was a Fabian Society pamphlet, called *Labour in the West Indies*, which gave an account of the emergence of the trade union movement in the 1920s and '30s and, more especially, of the violent confrontations between the unions and the government in the '30s. This was not a propaganda pamphlet. It was based on newspaper research and on conversations with some of the union leaders.

In London, meeting fellow anti-imperialists from all over the world, I launched upon a systematic study of the British colonial empire and its practices—color bars, prohibiting Africans from growing coffee in Kenya so that they were forced into the labor market to work for cash to pay their taxes, and all the rest.

But during the war one felt the atmosphere changing. Talking with many other anti-imperialists, especially British Labour members of Parliament, one got the sense that the powers that be had lost interest in the empire and were going to give it up. I was even invited by the Colonial Office in 1943 to be the secretary of a newly established Economic Advisory Committee. At my suggestion this committee launched on a systematic survey of economic policy in one sector after another, from which I learned, among other things, how much the officials disagreed among themselves as to what should be done.

In 1946 LSE set up a special course for social workers from the colonies, who were brought over for a year, and I was asked to teach them elementary economics. I made it a course on economic policy. I remember stopping a student who was in the middle of a passionate attack on the British governor of his country for some particular policy and saying to him, "But what would you do if you were the minister? Within ten years your country will be independent, and you will be a minister or head of a department. Reciting the evils of the British government will not help you. You will need a positive program of your own. The year you spend at LSE is your opportunity to learn how to face up to difficult problems." My dating was a little premature; it took seventeen years instead of ten for his country to become independent—but otherwise I was right, even to the point of his becoming a department head.

I give you this background because it explains something of the emphasis of my writings. I have always taken it for granted that what matters most to growth is to make the best use of one's own resources, and that the exterior events are secondary.

An expert on development should be able to give the minister practical advice. I do not adhere to this austerely. I am interested in historical processes and occasionally excite myself with the philosophy of the international economic order, but what I think about and write about most is domestic policy.

I began to teach development economics systematically when I went to Manchester in 1948 as a full professor. The emphasis was heavily on policy. One must therefore have a good idea of the sociological background and also of the political linkages. There are economists who put too much emphasis on prices, forgetting that it may be easier to solve a problem by changing the institutions wherein it is embedded than by changing prices. There are other, structural economists, who avoid the use of prices as a policy instrument because of adverse effects on the distribution and volatility of income. I am usually somewhere in between. One purpose of the book that I published in 1955, *The Theory of Economic Growth*, was to give shape to the discussion and to ensure that anyone interested in the economics of a problem would find it deployed with all its social ramifications.

My chief contribution to the subject was the two-sector model, advanced the year before. I arrived at this through looking at the distribution of income over a long period. I had read in the works of John and Barbara Hammond that the industrial revolution had not raised urban wages. If this was so, it would explain why the share of profits in the national income would rise, contrary to the expectation of the neoclassical economists that it would be constant. This constancy of real wages I felt to be bound up with another mystery. A number of developing countries had been developing for a long time: Ceylon, for example, for a hundred years. Why was the standard of living of the masses still so low? One could understand this for much-exploited South Africa, but how for fairly enlightened Ceylon?

The answer to both questions came by breaking an intellectual constraint. In all the general equilibrium models taught to me the elasticity of supply of labor was zero, so any increase in investment increases the demand for labor and raises wages. Instead, make the elasticity of supply of labor infinite, and my problems are solved. In this model growth raises profits because all of the benefits of advancing technology accrue to employers and to a small class of well-paid workers that emerges in an urban sea of a low-wage proletariat. In the commodities market an unlimited supply of tropical produce also gives the benefit of advancing technology to the industrial buyers, by the process already described.

This model attracted the attention of economists all over the world, because it applied in so many situations. One had to be careful that it did apply to the particular situation and use it only if it did. It was particularly useful in handling the problem of migration, which rose to significance after the war in most countries of the world, developed or developing, as people moved in vast numbers between the country and the town and from poor to rich countries. It is, for example, the way to approach the effects of mass migration of Mexicans to the U.S. or Turks to Germany. Add the population explosion, the element of technological unemployment, and the movement of women out of the household into the marketplace, and developing countries find themselves with a supply of urban labor too large for full employment. The wage level of unskilled workers then has upper and lower bounds that function much like an infinite elasticity of supply. Needless to say, absolute infinity is neither needed nor intended. The impact of the model is now greatly reduced. Undergraduates are no longer given models in which the elasticity of supply of labor is always zero, so the possibility that it may sometimes be nearly infinite is no big thing. Actually, several books and articles were written about it over the next few years, but the excitement has died down.

After 1950 I traveled a great deal in the Third World. This became possible because in 1947 I had married Gladys Jacobs, from neighboring Grenada. We are still together. She, too, was brought up on the Protestant ethic. She concentrated on making a home for our two children and me and took my absences on duty in her stride.

My visits were sometimes as an adviser, sometimes attending conferences, and sometimes for teaching. The role of advisers diminished steadily. When one visited a country in, say, 1960, having specialized in the subject over a dozen years and acquired a comparative knowledge of what was being done in different countries, one could almost certainly, when asked for an opinion, say, "In country X they are doing this and in country Y they are trying that." But by 1980 these countries employ numbers of professional economists well trained in economic techniques and policies. They may still be happy to see you, but they know much more than you do about their economic problems.

For my part I learned enormously from what I saw and heard on my travels. For example, I never joined the bandwagon for spending unlimited sums on higher education, partly because Egypt and India made me skeptical as to absorptive capacity and also because a sense of responsibility, during my term as vice-chancellor of the University of the West Indies, made me reluctant to ask the minister of finance for one cent more than I could justify. So my articles on education used the manpower budgeting approach, instead of the then elite but now discredited marginal productivity approach.

It was in Ghana that I first saw the results of excessive migration into the towns and started writing about it.

It was in Jamaica that I first discovered and wrote about what is now called the "Dutch disease." One industry, itself employing few people but earning a lot of foreign exchange, pays very high wages. This pulls up wages in other industries beyond what they can pay and so causes unemployment.

It was in India that I met the problem of the arid zones and discovered that hundreds of millions of people live on lands that are never going to yield a high standard of living. My book on development planning was based on practical experience in making development plans in the Caribbean and in West Africa.

I learned in many countries just how difficult the political problem is, in many dimensions. The simplest dimension is management: getting things done on time and more or less in the form authorized. Another dimension is the minimization of corruption, which is worse still when it is allied with nepotism and results in appointing incompetent managements. Finally, I observed that most of these countries are not homogeneous: they are divided by religion, language, tribe, or race. My book *Politics in West Africa* highlighted this issue and made proposals. It was hotly attacked at the time, but the analysis is now regarded as obvious.

Development economists can be divided into two categories: the gloomy and the optimistic. The gloomy subgroups do not necessarily agree with each other. Some hold that participation in foreign trade weakens the developing economy by destroying its handicraft industries or by sponsoring the demand for foreign goods. Others are concerned about multinational corporations. Still others believe that the poorest economies cannot get off the ground without financial help, which will not flow in adequate amounts. I have always been in the optimistic category, at first because I took it for granted that anything the Europeans could do we could do; but with the passage of time also because the speed at which developing countries were moving in the '50s, '60s, and '70s left no room for doubt that most of these economies, though not all, have what it takes.

I make the point to remind you, if reminder be necessary, that the study of economic growth is still in its infancy. Countries rise up and fall, and we are not in a position to predict which ones will do best or worst over the next twenty years. This is equally true of developed and developing countries. Economics is good at explaining what has happened over the past twenty years, but when we turn to predicting the future it tends to be an essay in ideology.

Between 1957 and 1973 I spent nine years out of the library in administrative office: at the United Nations in New York; as economic adviser to the prime minister of Ghana, Dr. Nkrumah; as head of the University of the West Indies; and as president of the Caribbean Development Bank. I learned very little of relevance to the theory of economic development (in contrast with earlier visits to India and to Ghana), but I did learn a lot about administration. I have published ten books and about eighty other pieces. I guess that if I had remained in the university I would have written one more book and a dozen more articles. Set this against what I was doing, which was to build up high-quality institutions, whose high standards would yield fruit of their own and also be an inspiration to others. Sometimes it backfires. At a party in Barbados I met a young accountant and asked why he had not replied to our advertisement. "I wanted to apply," he said, "but one of my friends said don't go to the bank because you'll have to work too hard." "I don't do anything to make them work hard," I said. "No," he said, "but you work very hard yourself and everybody else takes his cue from you."

Looking backward over my life, it has been a queer mixture. I have lived through a period of transition and therefore know what it is like at both ends, even though the transition is not yet completed. I have been subjected to all the usual disabilities—refusal of accommodations, denial of jobs for which I had been recommended, generalized discourtesy, and the rest of it. All the same, some doors that were supposed to be closed opened as I approached them. I have got used to being the first black to do this or that, which gets to be more difficult as the transition opens up new opportunities. Having to be a role model is a bit of a strain, but I try to remember that others are coming after me, and that whether the door will be shut in their faces as they approach will depend to some small extent on how I conduct myself. As I said at the beginning, I had never intended to be an economist. My mother taught us to make the best of what we have, and that is what I have tried to do.

Date of Birth

January 23, 1915

Academic Degrees

B. Com. University of London, 1937
Ph.D.   University of London, 1940

Academic Affiliations

Lecturer, University of London, 1938–1948

Stanley Jevons Professor of Political Economy, University of Manchester, 1948–1958

Vice Chancellor, University of West Indies, 1959–1963

James Madison Professor of Political Economy, Princeton University, 1963–present

Selected Books

Principles of Economic Planning
Overhead Costs
The Theory of Economic Growth
Some Aspects of Economic Development
The Evolution of the International Economic Order

Lawrence R. Klein

In studying the development of great economists and trying to understand why economic thinking takes particular directions, it has always seemed fruitful to me to look at the interaction, often one-way, between the prevailing situation of the economy and developing tendencies in economic thought. This has been most noticeable in macroeconomics but is also the case in the whole of economics. A primary example, which is closely tied up with my own development, is the emergence of Keynesian economics to deal with the problems of the '20s and '30s, especially the great depression. Keynes was intensely interested in the problems of the day and tried to develop an economic theory that would deal with these problems. It was long in coming. His career got a large impetus from the Treaty of Versailles, then the problems of the gold standard in England, inflation after World War I, unemployment, and the world collapse after 1929.

For our university catalogue, all professors are being asked to write a sentence or three about why they entered their respective fields. I entered economics because, as a youth of the depression, I wanted intensely to have some understanding of what was going on around me. It was psychologically difficult to grow up during the depression. It was easy to become discouraged about economic life and did not give one, at eighteen or twenty years, the feeling that there were boundless opportunities just waiting for exploitation. The young people of the past two or three decades have had nuclear war to worry about, but they have also had feelings of abundant opportunities if peace could be preserved.

But I was blessed with something else, that just happened. I was carrying around in my head the feeling that mathematics could be used in the analysis of economic problems. I spent most of my undergraduate time in either mathematics or economics classes. I was not a creative mathematician or any kind of a match for *wunderkinder*; I saw that readily enough in math competitions. But I was fascinated by university-level mathematics and had some hunches about applications of mathematics to economics, say, to the expression for demand curves and the estimation of revenues. It was a great surprise for me to go into the U.C. Berkeley library and find journals for a whole budding subject, carried out at an advanced level, handling problems that were far more complicated than anything that I had thought about.

My undergraduate advisers gave me no encouragement to study mathematics along with economics; I went my own way and took the best of Berkeley in the early '40s—first-class departments in economics, mathematics, and mathematical statistics. Of course, one can go back to high school or, in my case, junior college and find roots; there are some indeed, but my professional beginnings were in the Berkeley that existed just before World War II and the scholarship I won to MIT. There I met the dazzling *wunderkind* Paul Samuelson. When I was browsing in the Berkeley library and came across early issues of *Econometrica*, Samuelson's contributions caught my eye. When I got an opportunity to go to MIT, it was the possibility of working with Samuelson that confirmed all my choices. I was attached to him as a graduate assistant from the outset, and I tried to maximize my contact with him, picking up insights that he scattered on every encounter.

Working with Samuelson, who was at the forefront of interpreting Keynesian theory for teaching and policy application, I was put immediately in the midst of two challenging contests—one to gain acceptance for a way of thinking about macroeconomics and another to gain acceptance for a methodology in economics, namely, the mathematical method. Later, both challenges were to be overcome, but for ten or twenty years opposition was fierce.

Once Samuelson's *Economics* became a widely used text in first courses in the subject, Keynesian economics was firmly embedded. There was no turning back from that achievement. The successive student generations turned more toward the mathematical approach in graduate school, and they taught or did research in this vein. That eventually established the mathematical method, first in the United States, then in Europe, Japan, India, and other centers. Much of the foundation was built in Europe, and many of the American masters at mathematical economics were immigrants, but Samuelson, Friedman, and others gave it a native-born American flavor, and the approach truly caught on in this country.

The MIT years were, for me, a start in the professional field of economics, and my first position after leaving graduate school was with the Cowles Commission at the University of Chicago. Being just twenty-four years old when I started work there, I was almost in the position of having another chance at graduate school. As in many scientific fields of study, I was essentially a postdoctoral fellow.

A truly exceptional group of people was assembled in Chicago during the late 1940s. I doubt that such a group could ever be put together again in economics. From our closely knit group, four Nobel laureates have emerged, and two others came from the next bunching of Cowles researchers—partly at Chicago and partly at Yale. We worked as a team and focused on a single problem—to put together an econometric model of the American economy (a second attempt after Tinbergen's of the 1930s)—using the best of statistical theory, economic theory, and available data. After about four or five years of intensive research built up around this theme, the team dispersed to new openings in academic life. The effort was kept alive through my own research, and many of the brilliant people of our group went on to do their work in quite different branches of economics—Koopmans in activity analysis, Arrow in general equilibrium theory, Simon in decision analysis, Anderson in statistics, Marschak in the theory of organization, and so on.

In our attempts to bring together econometric methods and Keynesian analysis of the macroeconomy we felt quite confident. In the field of postwar planning we imagined that we had the well-being of the economy right in the palms of our hands. Over the coming decade we accomplished much more by way of model building and using than we ever thought possible in our wildest dreams of postwar America, but it was never good enough. We built systems that evolved from our teamwork at the Cowles Commission, and they have become part of the standard tool kit of economists. They play a very big role, but they do not dominate the policy process. They take a leadership role in forecasting, but they are not the sole survivors in the forecasting derby.

Scientists at Chicago were, secretively, carrying out more significant team research than we economists at the Cowles Commission. Because the director of the Cowles Commission was an old friend (from Europe of the two previous decades) of Leo Szilard, a leader among the scientists, we had a great deal of interaction. Szilard, one of the cleverest people of this century, dabbled in amateur economics. He constructed parlor games of the macroeconomy to demonstrate a scheme of monetary control that he thought would lead the world to a cycle-free existence. He taught us a lot about the strategy of intellectual research and the blending of politics and science. Many of us interacted with him and also with the amazing John von Neumann, who frequently visited Chicago on his way to Los Alamos. In those days, a trip across country involved changing trains in Chicago. Another visitor who had a profound influence on everyone at Cowles was Abraham Wald, the mathematical statistician from Columbia University.

The next phase of my career was to become more internationally minded. These days, some of us travel all over the world every month; European trips are almost routine. But when I left the Cowles Commission in 1947, I set out on an ocean voyage to Europe, after a summer's research activity in Ottawa putting together the first model of the Canadian economy. That project has survived many generations and gave birth to an active professional community in Canada that still functions on an expanded level.

Visits to centers of economic and econometric research throughout Europe were part of my education. I learned a great deal about the world, but was more attracted by the liveliness of the development of our subject in America. Seeing Europe dig out from the postwar rubble was a learning experience, and it opened many professional relationships that remain active. It certainly had a major impact on my own career development.

Before the war Cambridge, England, and London were the centers of economic thinking that shaped the world. Traveling fellows gravitated there for study. America had begun to compete, but from 1946 onward the magnet was the United States. Students came from all over to do their work in America. This was true in many fields and has not changed appreciably in the last forty years.

In that seasoning year abroad I made contact with the true Keynesians, the Cambridge group who worked directly with Keynes. I never met Keynes himself, but I got good insight into the group's thinking from Kahn, Joan Robinson, and Sraffa. I also met Kaldor and Stone on that trip. The interesting thing to me was that my teacher, Paul Samuelson, had inferred all that there was to know about this group without ever having been there. People in Cambridge remarked about this to me.

I had come to Europe for the first time only months ahead of Paul Samuelson and met him on his first stop—Norway— where I was spending most of the year abroad, learning from Frisch. Samuelson had just published *Economics* and was enjoying an early enthusiastic acceptance. He toured Western Europe just as I was completing my year there.

A problem with the interpretation of the Keynesian system was the influence of wealth on savings. In the literature of macroeconomics this became known as the Pigou effect, although Pigou had written about it more in terms of liquid assets rather than total wealth. People had emerged from the war with large holdings of liquid assets (especially government savings bonds), so it was a popular and important subject to investigate.

I had returned from Europe to join the National Bureau of Economic Research under the leadership of Arthur Burns. There I worked on production function estimation, focusing on the railroad sector, but after one year I worked jointly on a project with the Survey Research Center of the University of Michigan and the National Bureau of Economic Research to use the Surveys of Consumer Finance to throw more light on saving behavior, especially with respect to the Pigou effect.

One line of economic research that emerged after World War II was the one I was following in econometrics, particularly macroeconometrics. But survey research flourished during the war, as a tool to help government plan civilian activity in a way that would aid the military effort. One of the primary groups, located in the Department of Agriculture during the war, set up academic ties and formed the Institute for Social Research at the University of Michigan, Ann Arbor. I felt comfortable working with this statistical team. Also the cross-disciplinary attitude intrigued me. I learned a great deal about the interfaces between economics on the one hand and psychology, sociology, and other disciplines on the other.

At the Survey Research Center I learned a great deal about household behavior and techniques for measuring it. The work was based on samples of human populations consisting of a few thousand cases for each study. This initiated me into the realm of large-scale data processing, done by punched cards and electromechanical machines. Electronic computers were in existence but were not yet being used for most economic or social problems.

After I came to Michigan, where I was teaching econometrics on a small scale, but mainly concerned with survey research, I received some money from the Ford Foundation, which suddenly had found it necessary for tax purposes to make large grants of money available to several universities. Few people in the economics department had any ideas about how to spend the sum that was to be allocated to them. I then established the Research Seminar in Quantitative Economics, assembled some research students, and went back to econometric model building—restarting the research begun at the Cowles Commission.

One of those research students was Arthur Goldberger. He and I put together a new model of the U.S. economy called the Klein-Goldberger model. It streamlined the models built at the Cowles Commission, used some of the survey findings, and set about forecasting the economy on a regular basis.

Colin Clark, the intrepid Australian statistical economist, set us up for a great success. In the pages of the influential *Manchester Guardian*, which came my way in the weekly world edition, he observed that the winding down of the Korean War would possibly cause a large-scale recession. He frightened people about the most fearsome economic event of our time—a 1929-style collapse as a result of a cumulative downward spiral.

I looked at our model results for forecasts for 1953–54 and concluded that it did not look like 1929 again. I wrote a paper with Arthur Goldberger for the *Guardian* and was delighted to find that they would publish it, in large display accompanied by an intriguing Low cartoon.

In a piecemeal fashion the statistical work on the Klein-Goldberger model made use of the computer for parts of the computations connected with model estimation. For solution of the model we set aside a day or two of laborious hand calculation with a desktop machine. A large-scale digital computer was installed at Michigan, and we started a project for automatic model solution—simulation, if you like—but it was not quite brought to fruition before I was to leave Ann Arbor.

In the McCarthy era I left Michigan for the peace and academic freedom of Oxford, where I joined the Institute of Statistics and worked on the British Savings Surveys, patterned after the Michigan Surveys. While at Oxford I went back to model building, this time for Great Britain. My friend of twenty-five subsequent years, Professor Sir James Ball, attended my lectures on econometrics at Oxford and worked with me on the Oxford model. Some progress was made in using the computer at Oxford for more of the numerical work, but again it was not for model solution.

In 1958 I returned to America and took up a professorship at Pennsylvania, where I admired the position of the president, provost, and deans on the serious matter of academic freedom. From the beginning of my tenure at Pennsylvania and the Wharton School, I set out again to build a model of the American economy. This time I turned to quarterly data and, encouraged by my survey experience in England and Michigan, I used some *expectations* magnitudes. I started the first generation of a series of Wharton models.

The Wharton models shifted to a quarterly time frame, to emphasize interest in short-run business cycle movements, used more data on survey anticipations, and stated all the accounting identities in current prices. This last change corrected a defect in the specification of the Klein-Goldberger model. The first version of this new model was used for forecasting the American economy, and projections were sent round to economist members of the Kennedy administration, who voiced disbelief in the optimistic forecasts—recovery from the 1960–61 recession. Within a few years I was to turn my attention to a new approach, and I abandoned further work on this first version, but I turned over complete files, consisting of data listings and equations, together with a trained assistant to the Department of Commerce. They had asked me for help in starting a model-building project there. This evolved, with the help of other Pennsylvania Ph.D. products, into what is now the OBE model (Office of Business Economics, Department of Commerce). This model has taken off into its own life and is a distinguished member of the American family of models, but its roots are the first Wharton model.

At this stage I went in two research directions, each of which had a fundamental impact on my own professional development. The Committee on Economic Stability of the Social Science Research Council planned, in 1959, the creation of a new, enlarged, short-run forecasting model. I was one of the principal investigators of that project and played a role in designing a cooperative approach to model building, namely, assignment of a specialist to each sector of the economy. I undertook, together with other members of the steering committee, to fashion it into a consistent whole. In general, we had a model that was composed of the best practice in each department, and it functioned as a whole. But the real advances that emerged from this joint effort were (1) a detailed monetary sector that drew on Federal Reserve talent and was the forerunner of important monetary sectors in many subsequent models, thus repairing a defect of the Klein-Goldberger model; (2) an explicit input-output sector of interindustry flows that was tied consistently with the traditional macro models of final demand and income determination; (3) the preparation of a *databank* for the systematic accounting of all the data used in the system; and (4) automation of the computing for the project with a remarkable breakthrough in the ability to solve large systems of nonlinear dynamic equations. Other features of the research on this joint project have been outstanding and are documented in three project volumes, especially the final one.[1]

After the Social Science Research Council started the cooperative project, it was transferred to the Brookings Institution and became known as the Brookings model. In its cooperative set-up, we consulted many participants on its progress, development, and use. This was particularly striking in the case of computation. We struggled hard with the computer aspects among a group at the University of Pennsylvania (helped a great deal by our innovative young Ph.D. candidates, who prepared many of the first-generation computer programs for econometrics), a group at Brookings, and a group at MIT. I devised a clumsy algorithm at Pennsylvania; a suggestion by E. Kuh at MIT to G. Fromm at Brookings provided the essential link. When they communicated their findings about Gauss iteration methods, we tested them in Philadelphia and immediately switched to what has become a worldwide standard for solving large dynamic systems in economics. From the early days of computer application at Michigan, model simulation had been an obstacle to efficient model application, but once we saw the key principle, we were able to harness the computer for generations to come.

The SSRC–Brookings model was but one line of development, away from the first Wharton model. The second was to develop an entirely new model for a different kind of use—commercial forecasting. I secured a small sum from the Rockefeller Foundation for the construction of the first Wharton model. We then established a research unit at the Wharton School for general quantitative studies in economics, financed by the Ford Foundation and National Science Foundation. But I could see that these sources of support were temporary and would run out during the mid-1960s.

Meanwhile, several major corporations had independently approached me for help in their efforts at econometric model building to assist their economic research departments. I accordingly proposed to five core companies that we build one model for them at the Wharton School and provide forecasts in exchange for support of our research program in econometrics.

Michael Evans joined the Pennsylvania faculty in 1963 and participated in our new forecasting venture with the private sector. He brought with him a separate model that he had developed in his dissertation research at Brown University. At first, we prepared two forecasts, one from his model and one from the original Wharton model. After a short period a combined model was built, fused from the two, and this was the first to be published in a series of Wharton volumes.

The Wharton Econometric Forecasting Unit thrived. From five supporting participants in 1963 it expanded into a separate nonprofit corporation in 1969 (wholly owned by the University of Pennsylvania). It was sold in 1980 to a publishing corporation and was acquired by a French computer company in 1983. Both Data Resources, Inc., and Chase Econometrics took up commercial forecasting after 1969, and an entire new industry was born. It now has many competing firms and does business in the hundreds of millions of dollars.

With the growth of new centers of activity with models and support systems, it was natural to phase out the old Brookings Model Project. It had served its purpose and was superseded by the expanded commercial modeling systems and some fresh academic ventures.

During the 1960s the computer was finally harnessed for the needs of econometrics; it had first been used for scientific, engineering, and large-scale data processing (such as censuses). During this decade all those complicated calculations that we had contemplated during the development years of econometrics at the Cowles Commission became possible. I spent a great deal of time with student collaborators and IBM researchers working on nonlinear problems associated with maximum likelihood and other methods of statistical estimation, but we also perfected the simulation techniques that grew out of Brookings model research activities. We pioneered two developments that took econometric methods one step further: the presentation of results in standard national accounting form that were readily understood by users of econometric analysis and the use of time sharing. Data banking and perfection of time sharing were carried much further on a "user-friendly" basis for Data Resources, Inc., but the Wharton team had time-sharing facilities before DRI was founded. Computer developments were only started in the 1960s. They flowered in the next decade and became available to a large army of researchers and students throughout the world.

In addition to the standard uses of the computer for data management, statistical inference, applications (mainly simulation), and presentation of results in easy-to-read tables and graphs, many deep research techniques were developed, starting as early as the late 1950s. These were based on stochastic simulations, which involved the disturbance of dynamic model solution by properly drawn random errors. This research was pioneered by Irma Adelman in studying dynamic properties of the Klein-Goldberger model and by Harvey Wagner in constructing Monte Carlo experiments to test statistical techniques in econometrics.[2]

The Wharton team did not use these methods first, but we used them to good advantage to learn a great deal about the cyclical and inference properties of our family of models. Some large-scale stochastic simulations of the Brookings model had already advanced the use of computer-based experimental techniques, and we drew upon this fund of information. In this extended research effort, we learned to understand the various response characteristics of large-scale models—multipliers, sensitivities to parameter shift, and long-term trends of the system. The total computer effort of mechanizing the operation of large-scale models meant that the Wharton team was able to respond quickly and informatively to such major events as President Nixon's new economic policy, the oil embargo, and the fall of the Shah's government in Iran.

During my long stay at Pennsylvania several related efforts were conceived and executed in addition to the build-up of the Wharton models and their various applications to forecasting and macroeconomic analysis. Soon after I arrived, I became involved in a venture with two colleagues in Japan, professors Michio Morishima and Shinichi Ichimura, both of whom I had known in either England or the United States. We collaborated in the founding of a new scholarly journal, the *International Economic Review*. There were two principal objectives: to foster the development of modern (Anglo-American) economics in Japan and to take the burden off *Econometrica*, which had a large backlog of unpublished articles. In looking back at that venture, I would say that it made a contribution to the development of modern economics in Japan, although that might have happened anyway. We probably helped the transformation. We probably did not relieve the pressure on *Econometrica*, except temporarily, and we joined many other new journals in a virtual explosion of article preparation and the opening up of new periodicals. At any rate, the *International Economic Review* still stands as a collegial collaboration between Osaka University and the University of Pennsylvania, of almost twenty-five years' duration, and is now self-sustaining. In the founding years inexpensive Japanese printing, beautiful rice paper, and support from the Kansai Economic Federation made publication of the review possible. Those features are gone, but the review has a healthy existence.

The establishment of the review and other relationships took me to Japan in 1960 and on many subsequent occasions. In this connection, I prepared a model of the Japanese economy with Yoichi Shinkai and participated in a model project at Osaka University. Over the years, many Japanese models have rendered these efforts obsolete, but the research on Japan, together with the previous econometric research on the United Kingdom, directed my interest toward international model building.

In 1966 researchers at the du Pont company in Wilmington asked me to supply three models of developing countries where the company was involved in direct investment. Accordingly, I assembled a research team among the students of the economic research unit of Pennsylvania's economics department and prepared models for Argentina, Brazil, and Mexico. The company, as agreed, made their proprietary use of these models, but the system, complete with databases and equations, were, as agreed in advance, in the public domain. The research scholar for Mexico, Abel Beltrán del Rio, went with me to Monterrey in the summer of 1969. There we obtained a commitment from private companies for research support for elaboration and replicated use of the Mexican model in forecasting, policy, and scenario analysis of the economy. Within Wharton Econometrics we formed DIEMEX (Department de Investigaciones Econometricos de México). From a base of a few private-sector supporters in Monterrey and Mexico City in 1969 this has evolved into a self-sustaining system with some 150 supporters—U.S. companies, Mexican government agencies, international organizations, and others. What interests me most in this success is that the same technologies for model preparation, computer use, presentation of model results, and contributions to decision making in the private and public sectors could be fully transferred from our base in Philadelphia to a developing country. This is a prize case, but similar efforts have worked in many other parts of the world as well.

Starting with Latin America, I was able to foster model-building efforts in many developing countries. There are many models in the Far East, some in Africa, and some in the Middle East. Data deficiency has always been a problem, but that is gradually being overcome, and now practically the entire developing world is being modeled. Some of our best students had gone to various U.N. groups to work on problems of economic development among the emerging countries. I took on a consulting agreement in the mid-1960s with a group in UNCTAD to help them build models of LDCs in order to estimate capital needs for growth.

Parallel with model building for developing countries, a related effort directed at socialist or centrally planned economies was also initiated. The developing country models were deliberately structured to reveal some of the unique characteristics of these areas. They were not simply copies of models in the style of the neoclassical Keynesian synthesis that were being built for each of the industrial democracies (OECD countries); they had unique supply-side features, specialized foreign trade characteristics, distributional aspects, and demographic aspects plainly displayed. I had long been fascinated by the challenging problem of modeling the centrally planned economy, with its controlled markets and plan targets. In the summer of 1970, on the occasion of a lecture in Vienna at the Institute for Advanced Studies, I discussed these problems with economists in Bratislava who had contacted me in the United States. I continued these discussions during that summer in Novosibirsk and Budapest.

Finally, in 1973 I collaborated with my colleagues in Sovietology on a project to model the U.S.S.R. SOVMOD I and succeeding generations grew from that effort. In discussions and formal presentations, this model was put before Soviet economists, and I believe that by now we have a better understanding of that country's economic system. Visiting scholars from Bratislava, Budapest, Lodz, Novosibirsk, Moscow, and Beijing have, over a period of more than ten years, contributed to our appreciation of the fundamental differences in structure between the Western market economy and the Eastern command economy.

The modeling of the pieces—different OECD countries, some LDCs and some CPEs—set the stage for the next step, namely, the modeling of the international system. In a meeting of the SSRC Committee on Economic Stability and Growth in 1967 I suggested that we approach the growing international problem through a cooperative project designed, to some extent, along the lines of the SSRC–Brookings model project. Country representatives would take the place of sector representatives, and we could put together a consistent system of the leading economic centers of the world economy. The SSRC committee had earlier hoped to see such an effort undertaken by the OECD. We held a meeting in London in 1967 under the intriguing title "Is the Business Cycle Obsolete?" We, fortunately, recognized the continuing presence of the cycle, but were not successful in starting research on model building for analysis of the international problem at that conference. We did, however, establish some lasting contacts at that meeting that served us well for later developments.

With a small grant from the Ford Foundation, Bert Hickman, Aaron Gordon, and I assembled a group of international model builders from leading OECD countries in summer 1968 at Stanford, where I was giving some class lectures. We decided to launch a new project to model the international transmission mechanism. Initial support came from the International Monetary Fund, with active participation of Rudolf Rhomberg, and from the National Science Foundation.

This was truly a group endeavor. Many individual model builders from different countries and many specialists in international economics convened at formative meetings, realizing that there was a researchable project but not knowing exactly how to go about it. Through the dynamics of group discussion and person-to-person analysis, we finally decided on some procedures and goals. Out of that effort we spawned project LINK— *The International Linkage of National Economic Models.*[3] More than fifteen years later the project is still functioning and trying to break new ground.

At an early stage we recognized that the developing countries and the socialist countries would play an increasingly important role in the world economy. Although the main interest at the IMF was the analysis of OECD countries, the U.N. supporters of the project continuously pressed for attention to the role of the LDC and CPE areas. The project has grown from a system of thirteen OECD countries, four regions of developing countries, and one region of socialist countries to an enlarged system of seventy-two country/area groups comprising each of the OECD countries, most large developing countries individually, and most large socialist countries individually. That is the most ambitious coordinating task for model building that has ever been undertaken, and we are in the midst of putting all the pieces together now in Philadelphia. Each separate piece exists.

During the fifteen-year period of development we have succeeded in allowing for floating exchange rates, coping with oil price changes, adding country detail, introducing primary commodities, streamlining the enormous computational program, and tackling many policy problems through scenario analysis. Analysis of capital flows, coordination of policies among countries, and methods of optimal control are high on the present research agenda.

The computer, as one can easily see, has played a large role in my involvement with econometric research and application, but that part of the story is not yet finished. Interesting new developments are on the horizon. I am now involved in three research directions: (1) Use of the microcomputer for conventional econometrics. This involves collapsing the size of systems to fit limited, tabletop capacities, but these limitations are steadily disappearing. Some studies, especially of developing countries, are necessarily compact, small enough to fit the present generation of microcomputers. (2) Cooperative computing, whereby conventional computers are linked in a network for simultaneous computation; the LINK system is an ideal trial case. (3) Use of the supercomputer to accommodate the ever-increasing demands of the expanding LINK system, now consisting of more than 15,000 dynamic nonlinear equations.

Just as the Brookings model gave way to improved versions at the various commercial econometric centers, official agencies and some individual university centers, there is a possibility that project LINK could be eclipsed. The Federal Reserve System has their own multicountry model, as does the OECD, Japan's Economic Planning Agency, the Common Market, and Wharton Econometrics. What seemed chancy and questionable in 1968 has become an often duplicated reality for analysis of the world economy.

When I went to Eastern Europe and the U.S.S.R. in 1970, embryonic groups were starting up activity in econometric model building. I helped, where possible, and had many trainees at either the University of Pennsylvania or Wharton Econometrics. The same thing was true of activities in the developing countries. The case of the People's Republic of China is somewhat different. After the renormalization of relationships in 1978, I led a team of economists sponsored by the National Academy of Sciences, in fall 1979, to try to establish scholarly contacts. As a follow-up to that visit I organized, privately, with the Chinese Academy of Social Sciences, a summer workshop in econometrics in 1980. Also, visiting scholars from China have come to Philadelphia. Progress is limited but promising toward the preparation of a China model, maintained in the PRC, for LINK. We already have our own version of a China model built by Laurence Lau of Stanford University. A repeat visit in 1984 continued in the vein of teaching econometric method and trying to encourage participation in Project LINK. Similar workshops and efforts for LINK-compatible model building were undertaken in Taiwan during 1982 and 1983. Meetings with economists in Manila (Asian Development Bank and Philippine Institute for Development Studies), Bangkok (U.N. Economic and Social Commission for Asia and the Pacific), and New Delhi (Delhi University) are furthering the effort to have good LINK models for the whole Far East.

This account of forty years' research activity in economics and econometrics has avoided the political or the popular side. In 1976 I served as Jimmy Carter's coordinator of his economic task force. During his administration I tried to be helpful in various White House economic matters. I gave similar assistance to Milton Shapp, the governor of Pennsylvania, and W. Wilson Goode, the mayor of Philadelphia. All these private ventures contributed enormously to my own education. They taught me a bit about handling the media, about public appearances, and about the trade-offs between economic and political considerations. That experience was very interesting and I am glad that I did it, but I feel most comfortable in academia, doing the things I have described in this essay.

As for popularizing, I continue to write a periodic column for the Los Angeles *Times* and have had my stints at *Newsweek*, *Business Week*, and *Le Nouvel Observateur*. The *Manchester Guardian* in 1954 took my every word and table and published it as is.

The same is true in my continuing relationship with the Los Angeles *Times*, but I feel the same way about other popular excursions into the media that I feel about politics. The trade-offs with what I believe to be good economics are not acceptable, and I feel more comfortable writing in the scholarly domain.

Date of Birth

September 14, 1920

Academic Degrees

B.A.   University of California, Berkeley, 1942

Ph.D. Massachusetts Institute of Technology, 1944

Academic Affiliations

Lecturer in Economics, University of Michigan, 1950–1954

Senior Research Officer, Oxford University Institute of Statistics, 1954–55

Reader in Econometrics, Oxford University Institute of Statistics, 1956–1958

Professor of Economics, University of Pennsylvania, 1958–1964

Visiting Professor, Osaka University, summer 1960

University Professor of Economics, University of Pennsylvania, 1964–1967

Benjamin Franklin Professor, University of Pennsylvania, 1968–present

Distinguished Visiting Professor, City University of New York, 1962–63, 1982

Visiting Professor, The Hebrew University of Jerusalem, 1964

Visiting Professor, Princeton University, spring 1966

Ford Visiting Professor, University of California, Berkeley, 1968

Visiting Professor, Stanford University, summer 1968

Visiting Professor, Institute for Advanced Studies, Vienna, summer 1970, winter 1974

Visiting Professor, University of Copenhagen, spring 1974

Selected Books

The Keynesian Revolution

A Textbook of Econometrics

An Econometric Model of the United States, 1929–1951 (with A. S. Goldberger)

The Brookings Quarterly Econometric Model of the United States (with J. Duesenberry, G. Fromm, and E. Kuh)
Econometric Models as Guides for Decision Making

Kenneth J. Arrow

Studying oneself is not the most comfortable of enterprises. One is caught between the desire to show oneself in the best possible light and the fear of claiming more than one's due. I shall endeavor to follow the precept of that eminent seeker after truth, Sherlock Holmes, on perhaps the only occasion on which he was accused of excessive modesty. " 'My dear Watson,' said he, 'I cannot agree with those who rank modesty among the virtues. To the logician all things should be seen exactly as they are, and to underestimate one's self is as much a departure from truth as to exaggerate one's own powers' " ("The Greek Interpreter").

An individual examining himself cannot claim omniscience. I cannot really claim to know all the forces impinging on my life, personal or intellectual. Indeed, as will be seen, there are some elements in the development of my ideas and interests that I cannot now reconstruct. On occasion, on rereading an old scholarly paper of mine, I have realized that my mental recollection was in some degree in error. In effect, the speakers in this series are asked to be historians and biographers of themselves; and like all historians and biographers, they can occasionally make mistakes. Recollection can be taken as reliable when it can be checked against the documentary record. Otherwise, it is imperfectly reliable evidence, though of a kind to which the speaker, such as myself, has unique access.

I have always had an interest in the history of economic thought. In the last few years I have been giving a course in this subject. One question I have been facing is the relative importance of different factors in the development of new ideas. One might suppose, for example, that the personal histories and class backgrounds of economists would be important factors. Yet that does not seem to be the case. Among the great economists of the nineteenth century, David Ricardo was a highly successful businessman, a stock-exchange speculator to be exact, while John Stuart Mill was brought up to be an intellectual by an exacting father. Yet their economic theories were very similar indeed. Of course, access to education is important in intellectual development, and far more so today as economics, like all the natural and social sciences, has become a profession. Further, individual talents and interests may well govern which particular aspects of economics are studied and what techniques are used. But there is no evidence that the personality of an economist plays any significant role in the new concepts that he or she introduces to the subject.

I will therefore be brief in sketching my biography. My family, on both sides, were immigrants who arrived in this country about 1900 and settled in New York. My parents were born abroad but came here as infants, so they were effectively first-generation Americans. My father's family was very poor, my mother's hardworking and moderately successful shopkeepers. Both were very intelligent. My mother completed high school, my father college. My father was unusually successful in business when young, and the first ten years of my life were spent in a household that was comfortable and, more important for me, had many good books. Later, my father lost everything in the great depression, and we were very poor for about ten years.

I was early regarded as having unusual intellectual capacity. I was an omnivorous reader, and I added to that a desire to systematize my understanding. As a result, history, for example, was not merely a set of dates and colorful stories; I could understand it as a sequence in which one event flowed out of another. This sense of order crystallized during my high-school and college years into a predominant interest in mathematics and mathematical logic.

My primary and secondary schools were on the whole good. When it came to college, my family's poverty constrained me to attend the City College, which was then a completely free college opportunity that New York City had offered since 1847. I was far from the only able student in the same economic position, so that the quality of the students was high. The faculty, which was generally competent and occasionally better, was stimulated to hold the students to high standards, and I learned a good deal. Fear of unemployment led me to supplement my abstract interests in mathematics and logic with preparation for several alternative practical pursuits, among them high-school teaching, actuarial work, and statistics. It was the study of statistics that turned out to shape my economics career in a decisive way.

By following obscure references in footnotes, I learned about the then rapidly developing field of mathematical statistics, which gave a theoretical foundation to statistical practice and led to profound changes in it. When at college graduation, in 1940, I found there were still no jobs available in high-school teaching, I decided to enter graduate studies in statistics. There were then no separate departments of statistics and few places where mathematical statistics was taught. I enrolled at Columbia University to study with a great statistician, Harold Hotelling. Hotelling had his official position in the department of economics and had written a small number of important papers in economic theory. When I took his course in mathematical economics, I realized I had found my niche.

I received strong moral support from Hotelling and indeed from the whole economics department, somewhat surprisingly, as apart from Hotelling, economic theory was not well regarded by them. The emphasis was almost entirely on empirical and institutional analyses. The department's support was expressed in the most tangible and necessary way—good scholarships. As a result I learned economic theory as I had learned so much else, by reading. In my case at least, I believe this self-education was much better than any lectures I could have attended anywhere. The use of mathematics in economics had had a long history, but it was then still confined to a small group. By reading selectively, I could choose my teachers, and I chose them well.

I was an excellent student, but I was doubtful that I was capable of genuine originality. This concern was concentrated on the choice of topic for a Ph.D. dissertation. There were many possibilities for an acceptable dissertation, but I felt that I had to justify the expectations of my teachers and for that matter of myself by doing something out of the ordinary. This responsibility was crushing rather than inspiring. Four years of military service, though interesting in itself, served further to delay my coming to grips with my aspirations. Finally, a series of abortive research ideas, each of which seemed to be more of a distraction than a help, culminated in my first major accomplishment, known as the theory of social choice.

I will go into some detail about the genesis of this contribution of mine because it displays the interaction between the state of economic thinking in general and my own special talents and background. It differs in one significant way from the other areas of my research, which I will discuss later. The question was essentially a new one, on which there had been virtually no previous analysis. The others had been discussed to some extent in the literature, and my role was to bring new analytic methods or new insights. In social choice theory, I was almost completely the creator of the questions as well as some answers.

It had been argued by the more advanced economic theorists that economic behavior in all contexts was essentially rational choice among a limited set of alternatives. The household chooses among collections of different kinds of goods. The collections available to it are those that it can afford to buy at the prevailing prices and with the income available to it. A firm chooses among alternative ways of producing a given output and also chooses among different output levels. To say that choice is rational was interpreted by these theorists, such as Hotelling, John Hicks, and Paul Samuelson, as meaning that the alternatives can be ranked or ordered by the chooser. From any given range of alternatives, say, the technically feasible production processes or the collections of commodities available to a household within its budget limits, the choosing agent selects the highest-ranking alternative available.

To say that alternatives are ordered in preference has a very definite meaning. First, it means that any two alternatives can be compared. The chooser prefers one or the other or possibly is indifferent between them. Second, and this is somewhat more subtle, there is a consistency in the ordering of alternatives. Let us imagine three alternatives labeled A, B, and C. If A is preferred to B and B to C, we would want to insist that A is preferred to C. This property is referred to as *transitivity*.

Though this formulation of choice had been originated for use in economic analysis, it was clearly applicable to choice in other domains. Hotelling, John von Neumann, Oskar Morgenstern, and Joseph Schumpeter had already suggested some applications to political choice, the choice of candidates for election or of legislative proposals. Voting could be regarded as a method by which individuals' preferences for candidates or legislative proposals could be combined or aggregated to make a social choice.

The question first came to me in an economic context. I had observed that large corporations were not individuals but were supposed (in theory, at least) to reflect the will of their many stockholders. To be sure, they all had a common aim, to maximize profits. But profits depend on the future, and the stockholders might well have different expectations as to future conditions. Suppose the corporation has to choose among alternative directions for investment. Each stockholder orders the different investment policies by the profit he or she expects. But because different stockholders have different expectations, they may well have different orderings of investment policies. My first thought was the obvious one suggested by the formal rules of corporate voting. If there are two investment policies, call them A and B, that one chosen is the one that commands a majority of the shares.

But in almost any real case, there are many more than two possible investment policies. For simplicity, suppose there are three, A, B, and C. The idea that seemed natural to me was to choose the one that would get a majority over each of the other two. To put it another way, since the policy is that of the corporation, we might want to say that the corporation can order all investment policies and choose the best. But since the corporation merely reflects its stockholders, the ordering by the corporation should be constructed from the orderings of the individual stockholders. We might say that the corporation prefers one policy to another if a majority of the shares are voted for the first as against the second.

But now I found an unpleasant surprise. It was perfectly possible that A has a majority against B, and B against C, but that C has a majority against A, not A against C. In other words, majority voting does not always have the property that I have just called transitivity.

To see how this can happen, let me take an election example. Suppose there are three candidates, Adams, Black, and Clark, and three voters. Voter 1 prefers Adams to Black and Black to Clark. We will suppose that each voter has a transitive ordering, so voter 1 will prefer Adams to Clark. Suppose voter 2 prefers Black to Clark and Clark to Adams, and therefore Black to Adams, while voter 3 prefers Clark to Adams and Adams to Black. Then voters 1 and 3 prefer Adams to Black, so that Adams is chosen over Black by the group. Similarly, Black receives a majority over Clark through voters 1 and 2. Transitivity would require that Adams be chosen over Clark in the election. But in fact voters 2 and 3 prefer Clark to Adams. This intransitivity is sometimes called the paradox of voting. Of course, the intransitivity need not arise; it depends on what the voters' preferences are. The point is that the system of pairwise majority voting cannot be guaranteed to produce an ordering by society as a whole.

The observation struck me as one that must have been made by others, and indeed I wondered if I had heard it somewhere. I still don't know whether I did or not. In any case the effect was rather to cause me to drop the whole matter and study something else.

About a year later my thoughts recurred to the question of voting, without any intention on my part. I realized that under certain special but not totally unnatural conditions on the voters' preferences, the paradox I had found earlier could not occur. This I thought worth writing about. But when I started to do so, I picked up a journal and found the same idea in an article by an English economist, Duncan Black. The result that Black and I had found could have been thought of any time in the last one hundred and fifty years. That two of us came to it at virtually the same time is an occurrence for which I have no explanation.

Priority in discovery is the spur to science, and being anticipated was correspondingly frustrating. I again dropped the study of voting for what I took to be less fascinating but more significant topics, on which I made little progress. But a few months later I was asked a chance question that gave the problem sufficient significance to justify a reawakened interest. The then new theory of games was being applied to military and diplomatic conflict. In this application, nations were being regarded as rational actors. How could this be justified when nations are aggregated of individuals with different preference orderings? My earlier results, I realized, taught me that one could not always derive a preference ordering for a nation from the preference orderings of its citizens by using majority voting to compare one alternative with another.

This left open the possibility that there were other ways of aggregating individual preference orderings to form a social ordering, that is, a way of choosing among alternatives that has the property of transitivity. A few weeks of intensive thought made the answer clear.

Given any method of aggregating individual preference orderings to yield a social choice that satisfies a few very natural conditions, there will always be some individual preference orderings that will cause the social choice to be intransitive, as in the example given.

My studies in logic helped to formulate the question in a clear way, which stripped it of unnecessary complications. But I did not use the concepts of mathematical logic in any deep way.

This result quickly attracted attention. One by-product was that I learned from several correspondents of what previous literature there was. The paradox of majority voting had indeed been discovered before—in fact, by the French author the Marquis du Condorcet in *1785*! But there was not a continuous literature. There were some ingenious unpublished proposals for conducting certain elections at Oxford about 1860, based on the possibility of paradox. They were circulated by a mathematician named Charles L. Dodgson. Dodgson also wrote an adventure tale for the daughter of one of his colleagues, Alice Lidell, which he published under a pseudonym, Lewis Carroll.

The only significant published paper on social choice had appeared in 1882 in an Australian journal, hardly everyday reading matter. I know few if any interesting research topics that have had such a spotty and intermittent history.

The subsequent record is very different. The literature has exploded. A recent survey, not intended to be complete, listed more than six hundred references. A journal devoted entirely to social choice theory and related issues has been started.

Social choice is a topic in which there was little direct relation to past work, although the connection with parallel developments in the theory of economic choice was important. I would like to discuss two further contributions of mine, which illustrate different relations to current economic theory and to the world of economic reality.

The first of the two is the study of what is known as general equilibrium theory. This is an elaboration of the simple but not easily understood point that in an economic system everything affects everything else. Let me illustrate. The price of oil became very low in the 1930s because of discoveries in Texas and the Persian Gulf area. Homeowners shifted in great numbers from coal to oil for home heating, thereby decreasing the demand for coal and employment in the coal mines. Refineries expanded, so more workers were employed there. There was as well a demand for refinery equipment, a complicated example of chemical processes. This in turn induced demands for skilled chemical engineers and for more steel. Gasoline was cheaper, so that more automobiles were bought and used. Tourist areas accessible by road but not by railroad began to flourish, while railroads decayed. Each of these changes in turn induced other changes, and some of these in turn reacted on the demand for and supply of oil.

The economic lesson of this story is that the demand for any one product depends on the prices of all products, including the prices of labor and capital services, which we usually call wages and profits. Similarly, the supply of any product or of labor or capital depends on the prices of all commodities. What determines what prices will prevail? The usual hypothesis in economics is that of equilibrium. The prices are those that cause supply to equal demand in every market. This hypothesis, like many others in economics and indeed in the natural sciences, is certainly not precisely true. But it is a useful approximation, and those who disregard it completely are much further from the truth than are those who exaggerate the prevalence of equilibrium.

The general equilibrium theory, or perhaps vision, of the economy was first stated in full-fledged form by a French economist, Leon Walras, in 1874. But it was hard to use as a tool of analysis and too difficult for economists with little mathematical training to understand. Only in the 1930s did interest revive, especially through the masterful exposition and development by John Hicks, with whom I had the honor of sharing the Nobel Prize in 1972.

But there was an unresolved analytic issue, recognized by at least some. General equilibrium theory asserts that the prices of all commodities are determined as the solution of a large number of equations, those that state the equality of supply and demand on each market. Did these equations necessarily have a solution at all? If not, the general equilibrium theory could not always be true. Indeed, some work by German economists about 1932 suggested the possibility that the equations need not have a meaningful solution. A Viennese banker named Karl Schlesinger, who had studied economics in the university and continued to follow developments in the subject, recognized that the apparent difficulties rested on a subtle misunderstanding and felt that the existence of general equilibrium could be demonstrated. He hired a young mathematician, Abraham Wald, to work on the problem. Wald came up with a proof of existence under certain conditions not easy to interpret; indeed, in light of later work, they were much too stringent. Even so, the proof was difficult.

The heavy tread of history breaks in on the story. Schlesinger would not believe that Austria could fall to Hitler; when it did, he committed suicide. Wald did succeed in leaving and came to the United States, where he shifted his interests to mathematical statistics. He was one of my teachers at Columbia. I came to learn, I do not know how, of the unsolved or only partially solved problem of the existence of general equilibrium. But when I asked Wald about his work on the question, he merely said that it was a very difficult problem. Coming from him, whose mathematical powers were certainly greater than mine, the statement was discouraging.

As frequently happens in the history of science, however, help came from developments in other fields. The theory of games was in a process of rapid development. One theorem, proved by a mathematician named John Nash, struck me as being parallel in many ways to the existence problem for competitive equilibrium. By borrowing and adapting the mathematical tools used by Nash, I was able to state very generally the conditions under which the equations defining general equilibrium had a solution.

There was more than mathematics involved, though. It was necessary to state the general equilibrium system much more explicitly. As Schlesinger had already shown in part, the exact assumptions that were made needed clarification, and much was learned in the process.

As you may see from this account, the existence proof was based on general theoretical progress in economics and in mathematics, and I was certainly not the only one with access to it. Indeed, while writing up my results, I learned that Gerard Debreu, the Nobel laureate in economic science for 1983, had independently come to essentially the same results. We decided to publish the results jointly. Just before our paper appeared, there was one by a third economist, Lionel McKenzie, along similar though not identical lines.

Multiple discoveries are in fact very common in science and for much the same reason. Developments in related fields with different motivation help one to understand a difficult problem better. Since these developments are public knowledge, many scholars can take advantage of them.

It is pleasant to the ego to be first or among the first with a new discovery. However, in this case at least, the evidence is clear that the development of general equilibrium theory would have gone on quite as it did without me.

I may add that, despite their abstract and mathematical sound, existence theorems in general equilibrium theory have turned out to be very useful. They certainly stimulated many more applications of general equilibrium theory to particular economic problems. They gave a greater understanding of what may be termed "general equilibrium thinking," that is, recognizing that a particular economic change will have remote repercussions that may be more significant than the initial change. More directly, Herbert Scarf showed that the method of proof could be adapted to find a way of actually calculating the solutions to general equilibrium systems. The method has been used to study a variety of policy problems: tariffs, corporate income taxation, changes in welfare measures, and economic development in a number of developing countries.

The third contribution I would like to discuss is drawing the economic implications of differences in information among economic agents. My sustained interest arose from considering a practical problem, the organization of medical care, but the ground had been prepared by my studies in mathematical statistics, some of my earlier theoretical work on the economics of risk bearing, and some developments by others of these topics. My contribution here, unlike the first two examples, has been not so much a specific and well-defined technical accomplishment as a point of view that has served to reorient economic theory.

The general equilibrium theory, like most economic theory up to about 1950, assumed that the economic agents operated under certainty. That is, the households, firms, investors, and so forth knew correctly the consequences of their actions or, in some versions, at least acted as if they did. Thus, producers were assumed to know what outputs they would get for given inputs. Investors would know what prices would prevail in the future for the goods they were planning to sell.

I don't mean to imply that economists were so foolish as not to recognize that the economic world was uncertain or that economic agents didn't realize that this was the case. Indeed, some literature clearly showed that much economic behavior could only be explained by assuming that economic agents were well aware of uncertainty; for example, investors held diversified portfolios and bought insurance. However, a general formulation that would permit integration with standard economic theory and in particular with general equilibrium theory was lacking. I was able to work out such a formulation, which introduced the concept of contingent contracts, contracts for delivery of goods or money contingent on the occurrence of any possible state of affairs. In effect, I postulated the existence of insurance against all conceivable risks. My rather sketchy paper was greatly enriched and extended by Gerard Debreu. The idea was simplicity itself and yet novel.

It has become a standard tool of analysis, in this case rather more than I intended. I considered the theory of contingent contracts as a sketch of an ideal system to which the methods of risk bearing and risk shifting in the real world were to be compared. It was clear enough empirically that the world did not have nearly as many possibilities for trading risks as my model would have predicted. I did not, however, have at first a particularly good explanation for the discrepancy.

A considerable insight came a few years later. I was asked by the Ford Foundation to take a theorist's view of the economics of medical care. I first surveyed the empirical literature on the subject. My theoretical perspective suggested that there was inadequate insurance against the very large financial risks. Indeed, insurance coverage, both governmental and private, has expanded greatly since then. But I soon realized that there were obstacles to the achievement of full insurance. Insurance against health expenditures creates an incentive to spend more freely than is desirable.

Was there a general theoretical principle behind this? The concept of insurance against uncertainties did not fully reflect the actual situation, namely, that different individuals may have different uncertainties. The person insured knows more about his or her state of health than the insurer. The fact that individuals have informational differences is a key element in any economic system, not just in health insurance.

To take a very different example, consider tenant farming. If the landlord hired someone to work his or her farm, the farm worker would have limited incentives to work to full capacity, since the worker's income is assured. The owner could indeed direct the worker if fully informed about what the worker was doing. But his information can be obtained only by costly supervision. In its absence, the two parties will have different information, and production will be inefficient. The other extreme alternative is to rent the farm at a fixed fee. Then indeed incentives to the worker (or, in this case, tenant) are very strong. But farming is a risky business, and poor farmers at least may not be able to bear the uncertainty. Hence, the compromise of sharecropping arose. It dulls incentives, but not completely, and it shares risks, but not completely. Similarly, most health insurance policies have a coinsurance feature, so that risks are partially shared, while the patient still has some incentive to economize.

The theme may be stated without elaboration. Informational differences pervade the economy and have given rise to both inefficiencies and contractual arrangements and informal understandings to protect the less informed. My own contributions here were conceptual rather than technical, and the present theory is the result of many hands.

I have tried to present, as clearly as I can, the genesis of some of my researches. They have all been related to the present state of thinking by others. The field of science, indeed, the whole world of human society, is a cooperative one. At each moment, we are competing, whether for academic honors or business success. But the background, and what makes society an engine of progress, is a whole set of successes and even failures from which we all have learned.

Date of Birth

August 23, 1921

Academic Degrees

B.S.　City College, New York, 1940

M.A.　Columbia University, 1941

Ph.D.　Columbia University, 1951

Academic Affiliations

Assistant Professor of Economics, University of Chicago, 1948–1949

Acting Assistant Professor of Economics and Statistics, Stanford University, 1949–1950

Associate Professor of Economics and Statistics, Stanford University, 1950–1953

Executive Head, Department of Economics, Stanford University, 1953–1956

Professor of Economics, Statistics, and Operations Research, Stanford University, 1953–1968

Visiting Professor of Economics, Massachusetts Institute of Technology, fall 1966

Fellow, Churchill College (Cambridge) 1963–64, 1970, 1973

Professor of Economics, Harvard University, 1968–1974

James Bryant Conant University Professor, Harvard University, 1974–1979

Joan Kenney Professor of Economics and Professor of Operations Research, Stanford University, 1979–present

Senior Fellow by Courtesy, Hoover Institution, 1981–present

Selected Books

Social Choice and Individual Values

Studies in the Mathematical Theory of Inventory and Production (with S. Karlin and H. Scarf)

Public Investment, the Rate of Return, and Optimal Fiscal Policy (with M. Kurz)

Essays in the Theory of Risk-Bearing

The Limits of Organization

Paul A. Samuelson

Economics in My Time

The last five or six decades have seen American economics come of age and then become the dominant center of world political economy. When I began the study of economics back in 1932 on the University of Chicago Midway, economics was literary economics. A few original spirits—such as Harold Hotelling, Ragnar Frisch, and R. G. D. Allen—used mathematical symbols; but, if their experiences were like my early ones, learned journals rationed pretty severely acceptance of anything involving the calculus. Such esoteric animals as matrices were never seen in the social science zoos. At most a few chaste determinants were admitted to our Augean stables.

Do I seem to be describing Eden, a paradise to which many would like to return in revulsion against the symbolic puss-pimples that disfigure not only the pages of *Econometrica* but also the *Economic Journal* and the *American Economic Review*?

Don't believe it. Like Tobacco Road, the old economics was strewn with rusty monstrosities of logic inherited from the past, its soil generated few stalks of vigorous new science, and the correspondence between the terrain of the real world and the maps of the economics textbooks and treatises was neither smooth nor even one-to-one.

The great takeoff

Yes, 1932 was a great time to be born as an economist. The sleeping beauty of political economy was waiting for the enlivening kiss of new methods, new paradigms, new hired hands, and new problems. Science is a parasite: the greater the patient population the better the advance in physiology and pathology; and out of pathology arises therapy. The year 1932 was the trough of the great depression, and from its rotten soil was belatedly begot the new subject that today we call macroeconomics.

Do I refer to the Keynesian revolution? Of course I do. But people are wrong to associate with that name the particular policies and ideologies found fifty years ago in the writings of John Maynard Keynes, Alvin Hansen, Joan Robinson, Abba Lerner, and Michael Kalecki. The New Classical School, through the quills of Robert Lucas, Tom Sargent, and Robert Barro, reverse those Keynesian doctrines 180 degrees. Nevertheless, the present-day equations found in monetarism, eclectic mainstream Keynesianism, or rational expectationism are a galaxy removed from what were in Walras and Marshall—or in Frank Knight and Jacob Viner, my great neoclassical teachers in Chicago. The macromethodology innovated by Keynes' 1936 *General Theory* constitutes both the 1985 swords that slash at Keynesianism and the shields that defend mainstream macroeconomics.

So far I have been talking about the internal logic and development of economics as a science. It has been an inside-the-seminar-room survey of the subject, where of course the observations of the economic world have been brought into that seminar room. As a result of outside influences the period from 1932 to 1975 was a favorable one for economists like me, in that it was an epoch of tremendous university expansion and job opportunity. If one can borrow from the vulgar terminology of economic science fiction, my generation of economic activity was buoyed along by the great wave of a Kondratieff expansion.

The New Deal and welfare state created a vast new market for economists in government. Then came the war, which was carried on by armaments, cannon fodder, and economists: when the business cycle was put into hibernation by the wartime command economy, whenever problems of quantitative resource allocation ran out, economists could chance their arm on the new science of operations research, a game at which only the rare brilliant physicist could beat the run-of-the-mill economists.

Then came the postwar boom in education. Where there had been in 1935 only a few strong centers for economic research— Harvard, Chicago, Columbia, and a few others—now everywhere in the land there grew up excellent graduate departments. No longer did one wait to be made a full professor at forty-five; the typical new Shangri-La in the firmament of postwar economics was created by an activist department chairman, given the go-ahead signal by his administration to go out and hire hotshot stars at twice his own salary. Like beardless colonels in the wartime air corps, thirty-year-old full professors deigned to grace prestigious academic chairs.

Pax Americanus

The sheer number of American economists gave them unfair advantage over economists abroad. In addition, Hitler gave us even before the war the cream of the continental crop. Just as Chicago is the biggest Polish city after Warsaw, and New York the greatest Swedish city after Stockholm, America obtained practically the whole of the Austrian school in economics. Along with such names as Einstein, von Neumann, and Fermi go such American economist names as Koopmans, Leontief, Schumpeter, Marschak, Haberler, Kuznets, and many others. Later, as strength draws to itself strength, there began to appear in the

American lineup the names of Hurwicz, Debreu, Theil, Bhagwati, Coase, Fischer, and many others.

Again and again I have seen in recent decades the tremendous stimulus that top postdoctoral scholars from abroad have received from a year's sojourn in the States, hopping on the grand tour from Cambridge to Stanford. They go back home fired up to change the old world. For half a decade their reprints keep coming. Then, almost in accordance with some second law of thermodynamics, the Schumpeterian burst subsides.

Evidently science itself is not subject to the law of constant returns to scale. The book of Matthew applies: To him who hath shall be given. Unfair? you say. Well, as Jack Kennedy observed: Who said life is fair?

Life at the top

I have seen economists grow in public esteem and in pecuniary demand. Surveys have shown that the highest-paid scientists, physical and biological scientists as well as economists, are not to be found in private industry but rather in the university— perhaps in-and-out of the universities would put it more accurately. I don't know scholars who have agents. But some do have lecture bureaus. And being a public member on corporate boards has become a new way of life.

It is a heady experience to advise the Prince on a sabbatical tour of duty in Washington. Newspaper columnists from academia, serendipitously, acquire the omniscience they need for the job.

"And gladly teach" used to refer to the lecture hall and seminar table, but now includes telling congressional committees there is no free lunch and telling TV audiences to buy cheap and sell dear.

Trees do not grow to the sky. Every Kondratieff wave has its inflection point. The 1932–1965 expansion in economists' prestige and self-esteem has been followed by some leaner years. We have become more humble and, as Churchill said, we have much to be humble about. Economists have not been able to agree on a good cure for stagflation. That disillusions noneconomists. And, to tell the truth, it punctures our own self-complacency. We shop around for new paradigms the way alchemists prospect for new philosophers' stone. Just because a National Bureau paper is silly does not mean it is uninteresting. Just because it is profound does not mean that it is admired.

Mea culpa

So far I have been talking about economics. The title of this series, "My Evolution as an Economist," suggests that I should be talking about *me*. Mr. Dooley said that Theodore Roosevelt was going to write a book about the Spanish-American War called *Me and Cuba*. It would begin with Teddy's tribute, "My black sergeant was the bravest man I ever knew. He followed me up San Juan Hill."

I can claim that in talking about modern economics I am talking about me. My finger has been in every pie. I once claimed to be the last generalist in economics, writing about and teaching such diverse subjects as international trade and econometrics, economic theory and business cycles, demography and labor economics, finance and monopolistic competition, history of doctrines and locational economics. Kilroy, having been there, must share the guilt. (Goethe wrote that there was no crime he ever heard of that he didn't feel capable of committing. Bob Solow's reaction was that Goethe flattered himself. And perhaps what I called "crime" is a mistranslation of what Goethe meant only as "error.")

Here is my worst error. Do you remember the infamous wrong prediction by economists that after World War II there would be mass unemployment? I was not part of the multiagency team that produced the official 1945 forecast of doomsday. But, if you look at the yellowing files of the *New Republic*, you will find a well-written article by this humble servant that involves a large squared forecasting error on the downward side. My friend and mentor, Alvin Hansen, who believed in a postwar restocking boom, could have taught me better. And so could Sumner Slichter and a host of Keynesians and non-Keynesians.

I reproach myself for a gross error. But I would reproach myself more if I had persisted in an error after observations revealed it clearly to be that. I made a deal of money in the late 1940s on the bull side, ignoring Satchel Paige's advice to Lot's wife, "Never look back." Rather I would advocate Samuelson's Law: "Always look back. You may learn something from your residuals. Usually one's forecasts are not so good as one remembers them; the difference may be instructive." The dictum "If you must forecast, forecast often," is neither a joke nor a confession of impotence. It is a recognition of the primacy of brute fact over pretty theory. That part of the future that cannot be related to the present's past is precisely what science cannot hope to capture. Fortunately, there is plenty of work for science to do, plenty of scientific tasks not yet done.

Other testimonies

I shall not shirk talking more specifically about my own development as a scholar and scientist. But, as I do not believe in the kind of elegant variation that follows "he said," by "he averred," and then by "vouchsafed the speaker," I shall not try to duplicate some earlier autobiographical writings. Peppered through many of the technical articles in the four volumes of my *Collected Scientific Papers* are various personal reminiscences. But the richest vein of this kind of ore will be found in, first, my 1968 presidential address before the World Congress of the International Economic Association. It is cunningly entitled "The Way of an Economist," ambivalent words denoting both the economic road traveled and the personal style of the Siegfried traversing that road. Similarly, today in speaking of "Economics in My Time," I also mean economics in my own peculiar rhythms and style.

A second source is my "Economics in a Golden Age: A Personal Memoir," which appeared in the Daedalus book Gerald Holton edited, *The Twentieth Century Sciences: Studies in the Biography of Ideas* (New York: W. W. Norton, 1972).

A third source, one whose title was imposed on me, is *My Lifetime Philosophy*. This appeared in the series for students of *The American Economist* 27 (1983): 5–12, and will be in the forthcoming fifth volume of *Collected Scientific Papers of Paul A. Samuelson*.

The scientist delineated

Here briefly, in the third person for objectivity, is the superficial outline of my scientific career.

PAS has always been incredibly lucky, throughout his lifetime overpaid and underworked. A bright youngster, favored by admiring parents, he shone at school until the high-school years when he became an underachiever. The calendar lies in naming May 15, 1915, as his time of birth. Truly he was born on the morning of January 2, 1932, at the University of Chicago.

He was made for academic life. An A student at Chicago and an A+ one at Harvard, PAS wandered by chance into economics. Economics turned out to be made for him as the Darwinian genes from generations of commercial ancestors encountered their teleological destiny.

Every honor he aspired to came his way, and came early. He got the undergraduate social science medal his undergraduate year. Just when commencement loomed near, the Social Science Research Council created a new experimental fellowship program in economics, whose first award supported him handsomely at Harvard. Having drawn from Chicago giants like Knight, Viner, Henry Schultz, Henry Simons, Paul Douglas, John U. Nef, and Lloyd Mints, he levitated to Harvard Yard to learn from Joseph Schumpeter, Wassily Leontief, Edwin Bidwell Wilson, Gottfried Haberler, Edward Chamberlin, and Alvin Hansen. Before his SSRC fellowship gave out, he overcame the opposition of the Society of Fellows to economics and rode on the shoulders of Vilfredo Pareto into the sacred circle of Junior Fellows. The philosopher Willard van Orman Quine, the mathematician Garrett Birkhoff, the double-Nobel physicist John Bardeen, the chemists Bright Wilson and Robert Woodward, the polymath Harry T. Levine were his companions in arms in the Society of Fellows. There he hit his stride and began to turn out articles faster than the journals could absorb such quasi-mathematical stuff.

It is not true that PAS began life as a physicist or mathematician. Well into his undergraduate course he discerned that mathematics was to revolutionize modern economics. Proceeding to learn mathematics, PAS still remembers how a Lagrange multiplier first swam into his ken and how, with a wild surmise, it gave him independent discovery of the Edgeworth-Stackelberg asymmetric solution for duopoly—an insight that has kept him immune to the false charms of Nash-Cournot purported solutions.

His *Foundations of Economic Analysis*, written mostly as a Junior Fellow but usable later for the Ph.D. union card, won the David A. Wells Prize at Harvard. Later, in 1947, it helped him receive the first John Bates Clark Medal of the American Economic Association, awarded for scholarly promise before the age of forty. Its quality was thrice blessed: later still it contributed to his 1970 Nobel Prize in economics, the second time that fabricated (or "forged") honor was awarded and the first time to an American.

Hegira down the river

If PAS was born as a child his freshman year at Chicago, he was born a second time as a man that October 1940 day he succumbed to a call from MIT. MIT's force met no detectable Harvard resistance, so the movable object moved. It was the best thing that could have happened to PAS. A boy must always remain a boy in his father's house. On his own acres a man can build his own mansion and after 1941 PAS, along with magnificent colleagues, was able to help build up what became recognized as a leading world center for economics. Living well is the best revenge, Hemingway's crowd used to say; but, in sober truth, the example of MIT's Norbert Wiener, who in his days of fame still brooded over his ejection from Harvard Yard, led PAS ever to cherish his Harvard connections and labor for the greater glory of Cambridge and Middlesex County.

Peer recognition came early and often: from the American Academy of Arts and Sciences, the National Academy, the American Philosophical Society, and the British Academy. Just as it is the first million that is the hardest, one honor leads to another. After the first dozen honorary degrees, all it takes is longevity to double the number. The first such degree—from Chicago, alma mater and basilica of a church he no longer believed in—PAS found most touching. When Harvard honored a prophet in his own country, he also liked that.

Vice-presidencies and presidencies in professional societies came his way: the Econometric Society, the American Economic Association, the International Economic Association. As yet there is no Galaxy Political Economy Club.

A scholar at a new place for economic study like MIT receives plenty of offers from all over the world. PAS revealed a preference to be an immovable object, and when made an institute professor in 1966, with magnificent research opportunities and optional teaching duties, he in effect returned to the womb of a perpetual junior fellowship. Having arrived in paradise, he stayed there.

But not without excursions to the outside. Many a tutorial he gave to congressional committees. Often when he became a consultant to a federal agency, that precipitated its demise. The U.S. Treasury and the Federal Reserve Board did, however, survive his academic counsels. Murmuring that the United States is too precious to be turned over exclusively to big-picture thinkers like John Kenneth Galbraith and Walt Whitman Rostow, PAS gave economic tutorial to Adlai Stevenson and Averell Harriman; and worked his way as adviser to Senator J. F. Kennedy, candidate Kennedy, and president-elect Kennedy. Moses-like PAS did not pass into the promised land beyond the Potomac, but as an *eminence grise* he had the fun of backing the poker hands of such magnificent Joshuas as Walter Heller, James Tobin, and Kermit Gordon at the Kennedy Council of Economic Advisers.

What can the good fairies give the man who has everything? George Stigler, referring to Samuelson's 1947 *Foundations* and his newly published 1948 best-selling textbook *Economics*, introduced him with the words, "Samuelson, having achieved fame, now seeks fortune." Soon the smoke of burning mortgage could be sniffed in Belmont, Massachusetts. More than this, J. K. Galbraith's prophesy in a *Fortune* review, that a new generation would receive its economics from *Economics*, turned out to be right on the mark. PAS was heard to mutter complacently, "Let those who will write the nation's laws if I can write its textbooks." Being denounced by William Buckley for blaspheming God and man at Yale, the textbook took on a new aura of respectability and sales soared all over the world.

A quarter of a century ago the author of *Economics* commented on the new layer of fame that accrues to a scholar who writes a best-seller, stating modestly,

Writing a beginning textbook is hard work. But its rewards have been tremendous—and I do not mean simply pecuniary rewards. Contact with hundreds of thousands of minds of a whole generation is an experience like no other that a scholar will ever meet. And writing down what we economists know about economics has been truly an exciting experience. I can only hope that some of this excitement will rub off on the reader.

By joy possessed

Stop! Enough is enough. Of such *Who's Who* boilerplate, enough is too much. What has been described above could be said of many a successful go-getter. A West Pointer who hated soldiering might settle for a Faustian bargain in which promotions and blue ribbons compensate for a wasted life.

The reward that has counted for me in scholarship and science is the marvelous hunt through enchanted forests. I began to write articles for publication before I was twenty-one. I have never stopped. I hope never to stop. When Harry Johnson died, he had eighteen papers in proof. That is dying with your boots on! (Even for Harry, who never did things by halves or held down to the golden mean, eighteen was overdoing it.)

My mind is ever toying with economic ideas and relationships. Great novelists and poets have reported occasional abandonment by their muse. The well runs dry, permanently or on occasion. Mine has been a better luck. As I have written elsewhere, there is a vast inventory of topics and problems floating in the back of my mind. More perhaps than I shall ever have occasion to write up for publication. A result that I notice in statistical mechanics may someday help resolve a problem in finance.

Like a gravid spouse I achieve the release of publication. Have I published too much? Others must form their judgment on this. Speaking for myself, in my heart of hearts I have regretted almost no chapter, article, note, or footnote my quill has penned. And I have rued many an excision forced on me by editors of only finite patience or self-imposed for reasons of space and aesthetic measure.

Perhaps this betrays the lack of taste that marks the gourmand and not the gourmet? I hope not. I certainly sympathize with the view expressed in the following conversation of the classicist-poet A. E. Housman. A friend asked him why he was not including in a collection of his writings on Latin a certain item: "Don't you think it good?" "I think it good," Housman replied, "but not good enough for me." And not infrequently when I read some scholar's latest work, I have asked of Robert Solow what G. H. Hardy asked of J. E. Littlewood: "Why would a man who could write such an article do so?"

The able scholar with writer's block elevates by the mere passage of time the standards each future work must hurdle. It is easy to write a letter every day, but when you have not done so for five years, there is really nothing to report.

Repeatedly I have denied the great-man or great-work notion of science. Every drop helps, the old farmer said, as he spat into the pond. One does the best one can on the most pressing problem that presents. And, if after you have done so, your next moves are down a trajectory of diminishing returns, then still it is optimal to follow the rule of doing the best that there is to do. Besides, at any time a Schumpeterian innovation or Darwinian mutation may occur to you, plucking the violin string of increasing return.

Between Mozart and Brahms, I'm for Mozart. I am thankful for the precious gold pieces Pierro Sraffa left us. But economics would be the better if he had also blessed us all with some dozens of rubies and pearls. And, as I remember his eloquent but sad eyes, one wonders whether he would not have been the happier man if—as William James puts it—he had been born with a bottle of champagne to his credit. Maynard Keynes, who suffered from no writer's cramp, when asked at the end of his life what he'd have done different if he had it all over to do, replied, "I'd have drunk more champagne."

Earlier I confessed to having always been overpaid and underworked. Even good friends might agree with the first of these adjectives, but several will protest at the second, perhaps protesting, "Come off it, you work all the time, weekends and during vacations and, if legend holds, often during the reveries of the midnight hours." True enough. It is precisely my point though that working out economic analysis is play, not work. I am notorious for shirking tasks I hate to do. I minimize administrative duties, displaying an incompetence in their performance that chokes off additional assignments. Like Dennis Robertson, I always wash the forks last in the realization that should an atomic holocaust be imminent there may never be a need to do them.

If I am required to fill out an elaborate questionnaire, that liability is likely to stimulate me to write a new model in the theory of trade or in population genetics. Anything to put off the evil day of duty.

Remembered kisses

Novels about painters, musicians, poets, or scientists notoriously fail to convey what they do in the working hours of the week. Come to think of it, novels about allegedly great business tycoons similarly fail to capture what it is precisely that they do.

Therefore, speaking to an audience of economists, I should be more specific and describe some particular acts of scientific gestation. How did I first notice the problem? When did a breakthrough occur? What were the steps of development? And how, in retrospect, was the pattern of knowledge affected by the research?

But where to begin? I toyed with the experiment of describing the big ledger that, for a year like 1983, served as a partial diary of research doodlings. Thus, the January 1 entry might be jottings on how to devise a numerical example of a linear programming system that violates a crude version of the Le Chatelier principle in economics. This never got published. Yet. It refers back to work done in 1949, and indeed in 1937, when I was a student at E. B. Wilson's knee—or perhaps shoulder. One might then trace in the daybook a return on January

2 and 3 to the problem, and perhaps discern how it modulates into a related problem.

Suffice it to say that, in the course of a year, there will be half a hundred such finger exercises. But it would be misleading to believe that my 1983 research is well described, or even sampled, by the chance items that happen to get jotted down in one bedside journal. Therefore, I had better reserve for another and longer day detailed discussion of how some familiar result was conceived and came into being. (The impatient reader can be referred for a sample to my 1982 contribution to the Jørgen Gelting Festschrift, which I entitled "A Chapter in the History of Ramsey's Optimal Feasible Taxation and Optimal Public Utility Prices".)

Chasing the bitch goddess of success

Let me close with a few remarks on the motivations and rewards of scientists. Scientists are as avaricious and competitive as Smithian businessmen. The coin they seek is not apples, nuts, and yachts; nor is it coin itself, or power as that term is ordinarily used. Scholars seek fame. The fame they seek, as I noted in my 1961 American Economic Association presidential address, is fame with their peers—the other scientists whom they respect and whose respect they strive for. The sociologist Robert K. Merton has documented what I call this dirty little secret in his book *The Sociology of Science*.

I am no exception. Abraham Lincoln's law partner and biographer William Herndon observed that there was always a little clock of ambition ticking in the bosom of honest and whimsical Abe. No celebrity as a *Newsweek* columnist, no millions of clever-begotten speculative gains, no power as the Svengali or Rasputin to the prince and president could count as a pennyweight in my balance of worth against the prospect of recognition for having contributed to the empire of science.

Once I asked my friend the statistician Harold Freeman, "Harold, if the Devil came to you with the bargain that, in exchange for your immortal soul, he'd give you a brilliant theorem, would you do it?" "No," he replied, "but I would for an inequality." I like that answer. The day I proved that no one could be more than 60,000 standard deviations dumber than the mean, that Samuelson inequality made my day. The fact that subsequent writers have both generalized beyond it and discovered antecedents of it in earlier writings has not altered my pleasure in it. For that is the way of science, and sufficient to the day is the increment to the house of science that day brings.

Being precocious, I got an early start. Unconsciously and consciously, I was a young man in a hurry because I felt that the limited life span of my male ancestors tolled the knell for me. My father died young when I was twenty-three. I was supposed to resemble him, and the effect on me was especially traumatic. What I was to do I would have to do early, is what I thought. Actually, modern science granted me respite. Heredity, always, is modifiable by environment. Whatever the reason, I have been granted bouncing good health, a factor given too little weight in allocating merit to scientists and in explaining their achievements. A respected friend of mine, sometimes unfairly marked down as an underachiever, has been subject all his life to debilitating migraines. I say he is the meritorious one for having, as the Bible says, used his pound so judiciously.

There is another aspect to early, full (even overfull) recognition. It relaxes you. Why fret about priorities when, in the time you might spend in recriminations and turf claiming, you can dip your hook into the waters and be pulling out other pretty fish?

I long ago enunciated the doctrine that scholars work for their self-esteem, in the sense of what they all agree to judge meritorious. However, once your need for glory in the eyes of others has been somewhat appeased, you become free to work for your own approval. The job you will think well done is the one that brings true bliss. Perhaps part of this involves the faith that what one craftsman will like, so will eventually the rest.

There was never a time when I didn't strive to please myself. There have been those who thought that my fooling around with thermodynamics was an attempt to inflate the scientific validity of economics; even perhaps to snow the hoi polloi of economists who naturally can't judge intricacies of physics. Actually, such methodological excursions, if anything, put a tax on reputation rather than enhancing it. So what? Taxes are the price we pay for civilization. Such work is fun. And I perceive it adds to the depth and breadth of human knowledge.

At a deeper level one works not just to gain fame and esteem with colleagues. Not just to please oneself and enjoy the fun of the chase. At a deeper level the antagonist of Dr. A. B. Physiologist is not some rival physician at Göttingen or Oxford. The opponent is cancer. So at bottom is it with the economist. There is an objective reality out there that we are trying to understand, hard as that task may be. If ever a person becomes sick to death of faculty intrigue and professional infighting, if ever one sees democracy and civilization crumbling around one, always one can retreat to that objective study of reality. The complex numbers do not dissemble and even for toothache there is no better anodyne than five fast rounds with the puzzler of the business cycle or the intricacies of the theory of control.

I mean this literally and can illustrate what I mean by a true story. The late Voss Neisser, a refugee economist who graced the New School for Social Research, once told me what a relief it was in those grim days of Hitler's march toward power to grapple with the problem of the determining of Walrasian competitive equilibrium. I understood perfectly and agreed completely.

Someone asked me whether I enjoyed getting the Nobel Prize. I thought before answering. "Yes," I replied, "few things in life bring undiluted pleasure, but this one actually did." The honor was a pleasant surprise and came early, but not so early as to worry even me. Friends whose opinions I valued were pleased. If there were contrary opinions, I was too obtuse to be aware of them. My family enjoyed the Stockholm hoopla. Some colleagues in science have looked back with pain at the public interviews and turmoil that took them out of their laboratories. I bore up well and discovered that it takes only a few days of dependence upon one's own chauffeur to develop an addiction.

Indian summer
Sociologists of science study how the Nobel award affects a scholar. Do the laureates go into an era of depressed fertility? Do they write fewer or more joint papers, and more often list their names first or list them last? Does citing of them accelerate? What is the propensity to change fields—for a physicist to tackle the problem of the brain, for a chemist to become an expert on peace or the minimum wage?

To me it was a case where my cup runneth over—almost. The last vestiges of guilt disappeared when I chose to go off the main turnpike of my discipline of economics: to explore R. A. Fisher's notion of survival value, or Clerk Maxwell's image of a Demon who cheats the second law of thermodynamics of its certainty. I still monitor business trends and the latest fads like a hawk. I still write articles in the many different provinces of political economy. But the last generalist no longer feels it necessary to keep on top of—I mean try to keep on top of— all the literatures of economics.

As I veer toward the traditional three score and ten, how do I feel about it? Goethe, who like Wagner and Verdi had a great long run, wrote that the difference between age and youth was that in youth, when you called on it, it was always there in response. By contrast, only on the best good days could the octogenarian attain the peak performance. To myself, I am sixty-nine going on twenty-five. All the days seem as good as ever. But, as the lyricist says and reason insists, the stock of what's left of the good times must shrink as you reach September.

Date of Birth

May 15, 1915

Academic Degrees

B.A.   University of Chicago, 1935

M.A.   Harvard University, 1936

Ph.D. Harvard University, 1941

Academic Affiliations

Assistant Professor of Economics, Massachusetts Institute of Technology, 1940

Associate Professor of Economics, Massachusetts Institute of Technology, 1944

Professor of Economics, Massachusetts Institute of Technology, 1947

Institute Professor, Massachusetts Institute of Technology, 1966–present

Professor of International Economic Relations, Fletcher School of Law and Diplomacy, 1945

Selected Books

Foundations of Economic Analysis

Economics

Linear Programming and Economic Analysis (with R. Dorfman and R. M. Solow)

Readings in Economics

The Collected Scientific Papers of Paul A. Samuelson

Milton Friedman

The topic assigned to me was "My Evolution as an Economist."
I am sure, however, that some questions about the Nobel Prize
hold greater interest for at least some of you than my evolution
as an economist—in particular, how to get a Nobel Prize in
economics. So, as an empirical scientist, I decided to investigate
statistically what an economist has to do to get a Nobel Prize.

As most of you may know, the economics award is relatively
recent. It was established by the Central Bank of Sweden in
1968 to commemorate its three-hundredth anniversary. So far,
twenty-two people have received the Nobel award in economics.
Not one of them has been female—so, to judge only from the
past, the most important thing to do if you want to be a Nobel
laureate is to be male. I hasten to add that the absence of
females is not, I believe, attributable to male chauvinist bias on
the part of the Swedish Nobel Committee. I believe that the
economics profession as a whole would have been nearly unani-
mous that, during the period in question, only one female candidate met the relevant standards—the English economist Joan
Robinson, who has since died. The failure of the Nobel Committee to award her a prize may well have reflected bias but
not sex bias. The economists here will understand what I am
talking about.

A second requirement is to be a U.S. citizen. Twelve of the
twenty-two recipients of the Nobel Prize were from the United

States, four from the United Kingdom, two from Sweden, and one each from four other countries. This generalization is less clear-cut than the first because the population of the United States is more than three times as large as Britain, but the number of Nobel recipients only three times as large. So on a per-capita basis, Britain has a better record than we have.

A third generalization is, at least to me, the most interesting statistical result. Of the twelve Americans who have won the Nobel Prize in economics, nine either studied or taught at the University of Chicago. So the next lesson is to go to the University of Chicago. And I may say, in addition to those nine, one other, Friedrich Hayek, also taught at the University of Chicago for ten years. However, I have classified him as an Austrian rather than an American in my compilation. Beyond that, the statistics won't go, and that's all the advice I can give to potential Nobel laureates.

The most memorable feature of receiving a Nobel award is the week in Sweden in early December during which the formal ceremonies are held. It seemed to my wife and me when we were there that all of Sweden spends that week doing nothing but paying attention to the Nobel ceremonies. One party or affair succeeds another. The week culminates in a feast and a dance at which each laureate is required to give a toast lasting not more than three minutes to an already tipsy audience. I thought you might like to hear part of the toast that I gave in 1976. I will leave out the pleasantries that began it and ended it and give just the central part:

My science is a latecomer, the Prize in Economic Sciences in Memory of Alfred Nobel having been established only in 1968 by the Central Bank of Sweden to celebrate its tercentenary. That circumstance does, I admit, leave me with something of a conflict of interest. As some of you may know, my monetary studies have led me to the conclusion that central banks could profitably be replaced by computers geared to provide a steady rate of growth in the quantity of money. Fortunately for me personally, and for a select group of fellow economists, that conclusion has had no practical impact—else there would have been no Central Bank of Sweden to have established the award I am honored to receive. Should I draw the moral that sometimes to fail is to succeed? Whether I do or not, I suspect some economists may.

Delighted as I am with the award, I must confess that the past eight weeks [this was in December 1976] have impressed on me that not only is there no free lunch, there is no free prize. It is a tribute to the worldwide repute of the Nobel awards that the announcement of an award converts its recipient into an instant expert on all and sundry, and unleashes hordes of ravenous newsmen and photographers from journals and TV stations around the world. I myself have been asked my opinion on everything from a cure for the common cold to the market value of a letter signed by John F. Kennedy. Needless to say, the attention is flattering but also corrupting. Somehow, we badly need an antidote for both the inflated attention granted a Nobel laureate in areas outside his competence and the inflated ego each of us is in so much danger of acquiring. My own field suggests an obvious antidote: competition through the establishment of many more such awards. But a product that has been so successful is not easy to displace. Hence, I suspect that our inflated egos are safe for a good long time to come.

To turn to the suggested autobiographical subject matter, as I have thought back over my own life experience and that of others, I have been enormously impressed by the role that pure chance plays in determining our life history. I was reminded of some famous lines of Robert Frost:

Two roads diverged in a yellow wood,
And sorry I could not travel both
I took the one less traveled by,
And that has made all the difference.

As I recalled my own experience and development, I was impressed by the series of lucky accidents that determined the road I traveled. The first, and surely the most important, was the lucky accident that I was born in the United States. Both my parents were born in Carpatho-Ruthenia, which when they emigrated to the United States was part of Austro-Hungary, later, part of Czechoslovakia, currently, part of the Soviet Union. Both came to the United States as teenagers; they met and married in this country. If they had stayed at home, had nonetheless married one another, and had the same children, I would today be a citizen of the Soviet Union and not of the United States. That was surely pure accident, as it is for most residents of the United States, who like myself are the descendants of people who came to this country as immigrants one or two or three generations ago. As with my parents, most of them brought little with them except their hands and their mouths.

The second major lucky accident was a high-school teacher I had as a sophomore. His field was political science—or civics, as it was called then—but he had a great love for geometry. The course I took from him in Euclidean geometry instilled in me a love and respect for and interest in mathematics that has remained with me ever since. I shall never forget his using the proof of the Pythagorean theorem (the theorem that the sum of the squares of the two sides of a right triangle equals the square of the hypotenuse) as an occasion to quote the last lines of Keats's *Ode on a Grecian Urn*, "Beauty is truth, truth beauty—that is all/Ye know on earth,/and all ye need to know."

A third event, or rather series of chance events, occurred during my college career. As Bill Breit told you, I went to Rutgers University, which today is a megauniversity, a mammoth state university. In 1928, when I entered Rutgers, it was a small private college, though the process of converting it to a state university was already in its early stages, in the form of a system of competitive scholarships, tenable at Rutgers and funded by the state of New Jersey. I managed to win one of those scholarships, which relieved me of having to pay tuition to go to college.

My parents, like so many immigrants of that time, were very poor. We never had a family income that by today's standards would have put us above the poverty level. In addition, my father died when I was a senior in high school. However, thanks to the state scholarship plus the usual combination of such jobs as waiting on tables, clerking in stores, and working in the summer, I was well able to pay my own way through college— and indeed ended up with a small nest egg that helped meet the expenses of my first year of graduate study.

Because of my interest in math, I planned to major in mathematics. I was very innocent and the only occupation I knew of that used mathematics was being an insurance actuary, so that was my intended career. The actuarial profession is a highly specialized profession, which has an association that conducts a series of examinations that a budding actuary must pass to become a fellow and to become established in the profession. As an undergraduate, I took some of those exams. I passed a couple and failed a couple—the only exams I can remember ever failing.

By accident, I also took some courses in economics, and that is where the Goddess of Chance entered the picture, because the Rutgers economics faculty included two extraordinary teachers who had a major impact on my life. One was Arthur F. Burns, who many years later became chairman of the Federal Reserve System and is currently our ambassador to West Germany. When I first studied under him, more than fifty years ago, Arthur was in the process of writing his doctoral dissertation. Then, and in my later contacts with him, he instilled a passion for scientific integrity and for accuracy and care that has had a major effect on my scientific work. The other teacher who changed my life was Homer Jones, who was teaching at Rutgers to earn a living while working on a doctoral degree at the University of Chicago. Both are still among my closest friends a half-century later.

Homer later went on to become a vice-president in charge of research at the Federal Reserve Bank of St. Louis. In that capacity he has had a major influence on the spread of interest and knowledge about money in the United States. The publications of the Federal Reserve Bank of St. Louis are unquestionably cited more frequently in the scientific literature than those of any of the other eleven Federal Reserve banks; that is entirely attributable to Homer.

If not for my good fortune in encountering those two extraordinary people, my life would have been radically different, which brings me to the fourth accident. When I finished college I still didn't know whether I wanted to continue in mathematics or economics. Like all youngsters who need financial assistance, I applied to a number of universities for fellowships or scholarships. In the 1930s the kind of assistance a student could get was much less generous than it is these days—it was a different world altogether. I was lucky enough to receive two offers of tuition scholarships, one in applied mathematics from Brown University and one in economics from the University of Chicago. The offer from Chicago undoubtedly came because Homer Jones intervened on my behalf with Frank Knight, who was his teacher at Chicago.

It was close to a toss of a coin that determined which offer I accepted. If I had gone to Brown, I would have become an applied mathematician. Having chosen Chicago, I became an economist. As Frost said, "Two roads diverged in a yellow wood." I cannot say I took the less traveled one, but the one I took determined the whole course of my life.

The reason I chose as I did was not only, perhaps not even primarily, the intellectual appeal of economics. Neither was it simply the influence of Homer and Arthur, though that was important. It was at least as much the times. I graduated from college in 1932, when the United States was at the bottom of the deepest depression in its history before or since. The dominant problem of the time was economics. How to get out of the depression? How to reduce unemployment? What explained the paradox of great need on the one hand and unused resources on the other? Under the circumstances, becoming an economist seemed more relevant to the burning issues of the day than becoming an applied mathematician or an actuary.

The first quarter I was at Chicago, the fall of 1932, one course, with Jacob Viner, who was a great teacher, had a major effect on both my professional and personal life. Professionally, Viner's course in theory opened up a new world. He made me realize that economic theory was a coherent, logical whole that held together, that it didn't consist simply of a set of disjointed propositions. That course was unquestionably the greatest intellectual experience of my life.

In addition, it so happened that a fellow classmate was a beautiful young lady by the name of Rose Director. Because Viner seated people alphabetically, she sat next to me, and that too has shaped my whole life. We were married some years later and some forty-seven years later are still in that happy state. Again, consider the role of pure chance. Rose grew up in Portland, Oregon. I grew up in a small town in New Jersey. We met in an economics classroom in Chicago. Hardly something that could have been planned by anybody.

Other faculty members at Chicago included Frank Knight, Henry Simons, Lloyd Mints, Paul Douglas, and Henry Schultz. Economists will recognize their names; the rest of you will not. They were an extraordinarily talented and varied group of eminent economists. The graduate students were equally outstanding there—indeed one of them in addition to Rose is in this audience, Kenneth Boulding. I formed the view at that time, and have never seen reason to alter it since, that students don't learn from professors but from fellow students. The real function of a professor is to provide topics for bull sessions.

To continue with my own experience, Henry Schultz, who taught statistics and mathematical economics at Chicago, was a close friend of Harold Hotelling, a mathematical economist and statistician at Columbia, and recommended me to him. As a result, I was awarded a fellowship to Columbia. So after spending one year at Chicago I went to Columbia the next year.

Harold Hotelling gave me the same kind of feeling for mathematical statistics that Viner had for economic theory. In addition, Wesley C. Mitchell introduced me to both the institutional approach to economic theory and the various attempts to explain the business cycle, and John Maurice Clark, to his own inimitable combination of pure theory and social and institutional detail. At Columbia, too, the graduate students were a remarkably able group, some of whom have remained lifelong friends.

As a result of my experience, I concluded that, at least in the mid-thirties, the ideal combination for a budding economist was a year of study at Chicago, which emphasized theory, and a year of study at Columbia, which emphasized institutional influences and empirical work.

The following year I returned to Chicago as a research assistant for Henry Schultz, and once again chance was good to me. Two fellow graduate students happened to be George Stigler and W. Allen Wallis.

George Stigler is also a Nobel laureate and a fellow lecturer in this series. He still teaches at the University of Chicago. George was and is a delight and a treasure as a friend and an intellectual influence. No economist has either a more lively and original mind or a better writing style. His writings are almost unique in the economic literature for their combination of economic content, humor, and literary quality. Few economists have germinated so many new ideas and so profoundly influenced the course of economic research. Allen Wallis went on to be dean of the business school at the University of Chicago, then chancellor of the University of Rochester, and is currently undersecretary of state for economic affairs. Allen and George remain among Rose's and my closest friends and both have had a continuing influence on my own professional work.

The combination of influences stemming from Chicago and Columbia—the one heavy on theory, the other heavy on statistical and empirical evidence—has shaped my scientific work, essentially all of which has been characterized by a mixture of theory and fact—of theory and attempts to test the implications of the theory. I refer to "scientific work" to distinguish it from Rose's and my writings for the general public: *Capitalism and Freedom, Free to Choose,* and *Tyranny of the Status Quo.*

My doctoral dissertation grew out of a study I worked on under Simon Kuznets, another American Nobel laureate. Simon was then at the National Bureau of Economic Research. He hired me to work with him on a project growing out of data on professional incomes that he had collected in the course of constructing the initial Department of Commerce estimates of national income. The end result was a book Simon and I collaborated on entitled *Income from Independent Professional Practice.* The core of the book is the use of the economic theory of distribution to explain and interpret the data on the incomes of various professions. The book was finished just before World War II, but was not published until after the war because of a controversy about one of its findings. That finding had to do with the effect of the monopolistic position of the American Medical Association on the incomes of physicians—not exactly a topic that has lost interest over the subsequent forty-odd years. Similarly, a later book, *The Theory of the Consumption Function,* had the same characteristics of combining theory and empirical evidence, and that is also true of the various books I've written alone or in collaboration with Anna J. Schwartz on money.

Another major influence on my scientific work was the experience during World War II. The first two years of that war—1941–1943—I spent at the U.S. Treasury as an economist in the division dealing with taxes. Indeed, Rose has never forgiven me for the part I played in devising and developing withholding at source for the income tax. There is no doubt that it would not have been possible to collect the amount of taxes imposed during World War II without withholding taxes at source. But it is also true that the existence of withholding has made it possible for taxes to be higher after the war than they otherwise could have been. So I have a good deal of sympathy with the view that, however necessary withholding may have been for wartime purposes, its existence has had some negative effects in the postwar period. Those two years in Washington gave me a liberal education in how policy is and is not made in Washington—a most valuable experience. Fortunately, I escaped before I caught Potomac Fever, a deadly disease for someone whose primary interest is scientific.

The second two years of the war—1943–1945—I spent as a mathematical statistician at the Statistical Research Group of the Division of War Research of Columbia University. It had been set up to provide statistical assistance to the military services and to other groups engaged in war research. It was a subsidiary of the wartime-created Office of Scientific Research and Development. Harold Hotelling was its intellectual sponsor and Allen Wallis its executive director. That experience exposed me to physical scientists from a wide range of fields with whom I would otherwise never have had much contact. It also required me to apply statistical techniques to noneconomic data. Surprisingly, perhaps, it turned out that social scientists were often more useful than physical scientists in doing operational research that involved interpreting the results of battlefield experience. The reason is simple: social scientists are used to working with bad data and the wartime data were all very bad. Physical scientists are used to working with accurate data generated by controlled experiments. Many of them were at a loss as how to handle the data generated by experience in the field.

One episode from that period has contributed greatly to my long-term skepticism about economic forecasts and especially about econometric forecasts based on complex multiple regressions. One project for which we provided statistical assistance was the development of high-temperature alloys for use as the lining of jet engines and as blades of turbo superchargers— alloys mostly made of chrome, nickel, and other metals. The efficiency of jet engines and of gas turbines depends critically on the temperature at which they can operate. Raising the temperature a bit increases substantially the efficiency of the turbine, turbo supercharger, or jet engine. Experimentation was being carried on at MIT, Battelle Laboratory in Pittsburgh, and elsewhere. Our group advised on the statistical design of experiments and analyzed much of the resulting data. At one point in the course of doing so, I computed a multiple regression from a substantial body of data relating the strength of an alloy at various temperatures to its composition. My hope was that I could use the equations that I fitted to the data to determine the composition that would give the best result. On paper, my results were splendid. The equations fitted very well and they suggested that a hitherto untried alloy would be far stronger than any existing alloy. The crucial test was to hang a heavy weight on a specimen of the alloy, put it in an oven heated to a high and stable temperature, and measure how long it took for it to break. The best of the alloys at that time were breaking at about ten or twenty hours; my equations predicted that the new alloys would last some two hundred hours. Really astounding results!

A great advantage of the physical sciences over economics is that is possible to test such a prediction promptly. It is not necessary to wait ten years until experience generates new evidence, as is necessary with economic forecasts. So I phoned the metallurgist we were working with at MIT and asked him to cook up a couple of alloys according to my specifications and test them. In order to keep track of them, we had to name them. I had enough confidence in my equations to call them F1 and F2 but not enough to tell the metallurgist what breaking time the equations predicted. That caution proved wise, because the first one of those alloys broke in about two hours and the second one in about three. Ever since, I've been very skeptical of the economic forecasts that people like myself and others make by using multiple regression equations.

In my final comments, let me shift to a different aspect of the Nobel Prize in economics. As some of you may know, the establishment of a Nobel Prize in economics has been criticized on the grounds that economics is not a science. One of the severest critics has been Gunnar Myrdal, the Swedish economist who was awarded the Nobel Prize jointly with Friedrich Hayek. That was an alloy of a very peculiar kind—left and right. Myrdal accepted the prize, but subsequently he had second thoughts and wrote a series of articles condemning the prize and expressing regret that he had accepted it. Economics, he said, is not a science in the same sense as physics or chemistry or biology.

I believe that Myrdal is wrong. It is important to distinguish between the scientific work that economists do and the other things that economists do. Economists are members of a community as well as scientists. We do not spend 100 percent of our lives on our purely scientific work, and neither, of course, do physicists or chemists. In principle, I believe that economics has a scientific component no different in character from the scientific component of physics or chemistry or any of the other physical sciences. True, as those who believe otherwise often stress, the physicist can conduct controlled experiments and the economist cannot. But that is hardly sufficient ground to deny the scientific character of economics. Meteorology is a recognized science in which controlled experiments are seldom possible, and there are many other scientific fields that are equally limited. Economists may seldom be able to conduct controlled experiments—although some are possible and have been done—but uncontrolled experience often throws up data that are the equivalent of a controlled experiment. To give you a simple example, it would be hard to devise a better controlled experiment for comparing different economic systems than the experience provided by East Germany and West Germany: two nations that formerly were one, occupied by people of the same background, the same culture, and the same genetic inheritance, torn apart by the accident of war. On one side of the Berlin Wall is a relatively free economic system; on the other side, a collectivist society. Similar controlled experiments are provided by Red China and Taiwan or Hong Kong, and by North and South Korea.

No so-called controlled experiment is truly completely controlled. Two situations can differ in an infinite number of ways. It is impossible to control for all of them. Hence, I do not believe that there is any difference in principle between so-called controlled experiments and so-called uncontrolled experience or between the possibility of doing scientific work in economics and in physics. In physics no less than in economics, it is important to distinguish between what people do in their scientific capacity and what they do as citizens. Consider the argument that is now raging about Star Wars, the strategic defense initiative. Some physicists issue manifestos opposing Star Wars; other physicists issue manifestos supporting Star Wars. Clearly, those manifestos do not reflect simply agreed scientific knowledge, but in large measure reflect the personal values, judgments about political events, and so on of the physicists. Their scientific competence or contribution should not be judged by such statements. It should be judged by their scientific work. The same thing, I believe, is true of economists.

To return to my own experience, I have been active in public policy. I have tried to influence public policy. I have spoken and written about issues of policy. In doing so, however, I have not been acting in my scientific capacity but in my capacity as a citizen, an informed one, I hope. I believe that what I know as an economist helps me to form better judgments about some issues than I could without that knowledge. But fundamentally, my scientific work should not be judged by my activities in public policy.

In introducing me, Bill Breit referred to my wanting to be judged by my peers. The episode he referred to occurred in a parking lot in Detroit. The morning on which it was announced that I had been awarded the Nobel Prize, I had agreed to go to Michigan to barnstorm on behalf of a proposed amendment to the state constitution requiring a balanced budget and limiting spending. I had to leave Chicago very early. In Detroit I was picked up at the airport by some of the people running the Michigan campaign and taken to the Detroit Press Club, for a press conference before we started our day of barnstorming. When we got to the parking lot of the press club, we were astonished to see how many reporters and TV people were there, and I remarked that I was amazed that the attempt to get an amendment was receiving so much attention. As I stepped out of the car, a reporter stuck a microphone in my face and said, "What do you think about getting the prize?" I said, "What prize?" He said, "The Nobel Prize." Naturally, I expressed my pleasure at the information. The reporter then said, "Do you regard this as the pinnacle of your career?" or something to that effect, and I said no. I said I was more interested in what my fellow economists would say about my work fifty years from now than about what seven Swedes might say about my work now.

When I was barnstorming that state, I wasn't doing it as a scientist; I was doing it as a citizen deeply concerned about a public issue. Similarly, when I engage in activities to promote a federal constitutional amendment to balance the budget and limit spending, I'm doing so as a citizen.

The public has the impression that economists never agree. They have the impression that if three economists are in a room they will get at least four opinions. That is false. If scientific issues are separated from policy and value issues, there is widespread agreement among economists whatever their political views. Over and over again I have been in a group that includes both economists and practitioners of other disciplines. Let a discussion start about almost anything and, in ten minutes or so, you will find all the economists on the same side against all the rest—whether the economists are on the left or on the right or in the middle.

I have great doubts about whether Nobel Prizes as a whole do any good, but I believe that such doubts apply equally to Nobel Prizes in physics as to Nobel Prizes in economics.

I have wandered over much terrain and I am not sure that I have explained my evolution as an economist. Let me only say in closing that my life as an economist has been the source of much pleasure and satisfaction. It's a fascinating discipline. What makes it most fascinating is that its fundamental principles are so simple that they can be written on one page, that anybody can understand them, and yet that very few do.

Date of Birth

July 31, 1912

Academic Degrees

B.A.   Rutgers University, 1932
M.A.   University of Chicago, 1933
Ph.D. Columbia University, 1946

Academic Affiliations

Part-time Lecturer, Columbia University, 1937–1940

Visiting Professor of Economics, University of Wisconsin, 1940–41

Associate Professor of Economics and Business Administration, University of Minnesota, 1945–46

Associate Professor of Economics, 1946–1948, Professor of Economics 1948–1963, Paul Snowden Russell Distinguished Service Professor of Economics 1963–1982, University of Chicago

Visiting Fulbright Lecturer, Cambridge University, 1953–54

Wesley Clair Mitchell Visiting Research Professor, Columbia University, 1964–65

Visiting Professor, UCLA, winter quarter, 1967

Visiting Professor, University of Hawaii, winter quarter, 1972

Senior Research Fellow, Hoover Institute (Stanford), present

Selected Books

Essays in Positive Economics

A Theory of the Consumption Function

Capitalism and Freedom

Price Theory: A Provisional Text

A Monetary History of the United States, 1867–1960
(with Anna J. Schwartz)

George J. Stigler

It is a good rule that a scientist has only one chance to become successful in influencing his science, and that is when he influences his contemporaries. If he is not heeded by his contemporaries, he has lost his chance: brilliant work that is exhumed by a later generation may make the neglected scientist famous, but it will not have made him important. Gossen was a genius, but nothing in the development of utility theory is different for his having lived. Cournot was a genius, and perhaps a bit of his work rubbed off on Edgeworth and later writers on oligopoly, but the theory of the subject dates from the 1880s, not from when he published it in 1838.

Contemporary fame does not ensure lasting fame—the leaders of what prove to be scientific fads recede from even the histories of the science. Today a young economist will not know that a stagnation thesis concerning the American economy was widely discussed in the late 1930s, and Alvin Hansen's name will never regain its onetime prominence. Even Edward Chamberlin's theory of monopolistic competition, it is now clear, failed to initiate a fundamentally new direction of economic theorizing.

So scientific creativity—successful, lasting creativity—must be recognized at the time or it becomes a personal rather than a social achievement. This series of lectures is presented by economists who have met at least the requirement that their work has been recognized by contemporaries. A later age will separate the fundamental from the faddish contributions.

The conditions for creativity in economics have changed in one absolutely basic respect in the last hundred years or so. Until as late as the 1870s or 1880s it was possible for an amateur to become an influential economist; today it is almost inconceivable that major contributions could come from a noneconomist. The knowledge of economics possessed by Adam Smith, or David Ricardo, or even Leon Walras and Francis Edgeworth, was self-taught: they had not received formal training in the subject. In more or less modern times the only influential noneconomists I can name are Ramsey, Hotelling, and von Neumann; of course, each was a highly trained mathematician, and all date back forty or more years.

So to understand the conditions under which modern work in economics has emerged, one must look at the conditions of training and work of the modern scholar. Those conditions are no substitute for creativity, but they have become an indispensable condition for creativity to be exercised. I turn, therefore, to a semi-autobiographical sketch of my own life in economics, with primary attention to how the conditions of training and work influence the problems and methods of economic research.

Some autobiography

I grew up in Seattle, attended schools there through a BBA degree at the University of Washington, proceeded to an MBA on the downtown Chicago campus of Northwestern University, spent one more year dodging unemployment at the University of Washington, and then went to the University of Chicago to get a Ph.D. That breathless sentence covers twenty-two years, on which I shall elaborate a bit. My father and mother migrated to the United States from Bavaria and Hungary, respectively. My father, whose skills as a brewer were devalued by Prohibition, went into the business of buying, repairing, and reselling residential property in Seattle during its depressed 1920s as well as the 1930s. I was a fully relaxed student before college days, a voracious and promiscuous reader but not a strong scholar. At the University of Washington I did very well in classes, but usually chose the wrong classes. Lacking good judgment as well as guidance from my parents, whose formal education had been modest, I took innumerable "applied" business courses and a good deal of political science, but nothing in mathematics or the physical sciences. I was unknowingly providing proof of a proposition I have come to believe: that undergraduate training is to graduate training perhaps as 1 is to 8 in the acquisition of a research-level mastery of a field. Washington had some respectable economists but none who was at the first level.

Northwestern University began to open my eyes. I took, again, too many applied courses, this time chiefly in urban land economics. I studied with one able and stimulating economist, Coleman Woodbury, and he did as much as anyone to arouse my interest in scholarship as a career. But the University of Chicago was receiving pretty close to a tabula rasa in 1933, when I enrolled. Not that I knew it: twenty-two is not an age of humility.

There I met and got to know three economists I still consider to be outstanding: Frank Knight and Henry Simons, and a year later, on his return from the U.S. Treasury, Jacob Viner.

Knight was both a great and an absurd teacher. The absurdity was documented by his utterly disorganized teaching, with constant change of subject and yet insistent repetition of arguments. In the course on the history of economics he was interested mostly in the seamy side of religious history, but got great relish out of emphasizing the perversities and blunders of Ricardo and other historic figures in economics. His greatness is attested best by the fact that almost all of the students were much influenced by him. He communicated beyond any possible confusion the message that intellectual inquiry was a sacred calling, excruciatingly difficult for even the best of scholars to pursue with complete fidelity to truth and evidence.

Henry Simons was Frank Knight's disciple, but his example was enough to teach us that a disciple may have an independent mind, an ambivalent attitude toward some of his master's beliefs, and a wholly different goal in life. Simons believed that in the 1930s the world was at a crisis of historic magnitude: the survival of freedom and the economic viability of the Western world were at stake. With a wider perspective, Knight believed that the history of man was a history of social folly; the then-current crises were grave, but had equally grave precedents and would be handled as badly as they had been previously. Simons believed with all his heart that the crisis of the 1930s had to be handled well or the basic values of civilization would be lost, and he dedicated his life to that task.

One thing that Knight and Simons both succeeded in teaching me, and in fact overtaught, was that great reputation and high office deserve little respect in scientific work. We were told to listen to the argument and look at the evidence, but ignore the position, degrees, and age of the speaker. This studied irreverence toward authority had a special slant: contemporary ideas were to be treated even more skeptically than those of earlier periods. I didn't realize this distinction at the time because it was implicit rather than explicit. We were taught by example that Ricardo's errors and Marshall's foibles deserved more careful and thorough attention than the nonsense or froth of the day. One can make a case for the greater respect for earlier economists on the basis of the fact that their work had stood the test of time, but that case was not made explicitly.

When Viner returned to Chicago the next year we met a very different type of scholar: immensely erudite, rigorous and systematic in his instruction. Viner was the founder of the Chicago tradition of detailed training in neoclassical microeconomics, including training in its application to real problems. Viner filled the class of Economics 301 with a respect bordering on terror. I still recall the time when he asked a student to list the factors determining the elasticity of demand for a commodity. The student began well enough but soon put the conditions of supply in the list of determinants of demand elasticity. Viner calmly said, "Mr. X, you do not belong in this class." This remark produced a suitable tension in the rest of us. Yet outside the classroom he was kind and helpful, and my appreciation of him has risen steadily over time.

Among the very able people I met in Chicago were several students, and of course we knew each other in a way one could not know the professors. My special friends were Milton Friedman and Allen Wallis. It did not take long to recognize Milton's talents: he was logical, perceptive, quick to understand one's arguments—and quick to find their weaknesses. Friedman has surely exercised one of the major intellectual influences upon me throughout my life.

Allen Wallis was so competent and systematic that we soon predicted, to his annoyance, that he would become a university president. A year later Paul Samuelson appeared as a senior in some of our graduate classes, and we had no difficulty in recognizing his quality. The give-and-take among us students (a group that included Kenneth Boulding and Sune Carlson) was the first experience I had of constant exchanges in a circle of first-class minds, and I acquired a lifelong taste for it.

I wrote my dissertation in the history of economic thought under Knight. He was the soul of kindness and generosity in dealing with me, then and forever after, but in retrospect there was a fly in the ointment. He was so strong-minded and so critical a student of the literature that it was a good many years before I could read the economic classics through my eyes instead of his. I have never brought myself to read through my doctoral dissertation, *Production and Distribution Theories: The Formative Period*, because I knew I would be embarrassed by both its Knightian excesses and its immaturity.

So when I left Chicago in 1936 to begin teaching at Iowa State College, I had acquired a light smattering of mathematics, a partial command of price theory, a fondness for intellectual history, and an irreverence toward prevailing ideas bordering on congenital skepticism. In retrospect a most modest intellectual arsenal.

Iowa and Minnesota and later

At times I found myself in the midst of a group of vigorous young economists, who were being brought together by Theodore W. Schultz. I still remember my first class, in economic principles. I had prepared the first few weeks of the course in outline, so I entered the class with confidence. Forty minutes later I had covered all the material in my outline, and there remained ten minutes, not to mention ten and a half weeks, still to go! I wish I could state that eventually I encountered the problem so often reported by colleagues, of never being able to cover all the material, but I never reached this utopia of knowledge or loquacity.

I spent most of my spare time at Ames finishing my doctoral thesis, and I received my Ph.D. in the spring of the second year. I had a number of excellent colleagues and students at Ames, but before I was well settled in, Frederic Garver invited me to come to Minnesota, and I accepted.

My closest colleagues at Minnesota were Garver, Francis Boddy, and Arthur Marget. Alvin Hansen had just gone to Harvard and indeed it was largely his classes, but not his rank or salary, that I had inherited. It was rumored that my main rival had been Oskar Morgenstern; if that was true, I have fantasized that if he had been chosen I might have become the junior author of the theory of games!

By 1942 the outbreak of war led to a general retrenchment of academic life, and I took a sustained leave of absence from Minnesota, first to the National Bureau of Economic Research. I was hired to study the service industries as part of a program of studies of the trend of the output, employment, and productivity in the American economy. I and my associates collected an awful lot of numbers and published some monographs on such exotic fields as domestic science, education, trade, and (later) scientific personnel. These works were mostly quantitative, with mildly analytical skeletons, as when I made the first productivity measures relating output to an index of *all* inputs.

At the bureau I got to know Arthur Burns, Solomon Fabricant, and Geoffrey Moore. From them, and even more from Milton Friedman, I became persuaded of the importance of empirical evidence in the appraisal of economic theories; that is a theme to which I will return later. From the bureau I went to the Statistical Research Group at Columbia University, where statistical analysis was being used on military problems. The director was Allen Wallis, and the senior figures included Harold Hotelling, Milton Friedman, Jacob Wolfowitz, and, among other statisticians, L. J. Savage and Abraham Wald. I learned a little statistics there, and I did not seriously delay our nation's victory.

Near the end of the war I returned to Minnesota, and a year later Milton Friedman joined us. The reunion, alas, was brief, for a year later Friedman went to Chicago, and I to Brown. (I may mention that in 1946 I was offered a Chicago professorship, but managed to alienate the president, Ernest Colwell, in an interview and was vetoed. Thereby I probably hastened Friedman's return to Chicago by a year, and can claim some credit for helping found the new Chicago school.) And a year after that, I went to Columbia University, where Albert Hart, William Vickrey, and I taught the graduate theory course. I also assumed the teaching of industrial organization and the history of economics. Columbia then, as now, had a strong department, which included Arthur F. Burns, Carl Shoup, Ragnar Nurkse, and others. And that speedy journey brings me back to Chicago in 1958.

Back to Chicago

I was returning to an economics community in a stage of high prosperity. Friedman was an ascendant figure in world economics: his *Consumption Function* had revolutionized the statistical analysis of economic data, and his work on monetarism constituted the major attack on the ruling Keynesian doctrine. Modern labor economics was being fashioned by Gregg Lewis and by a recent Chicago Ph.D. already at Columbia, Gary Becker, and his colleague Jacob Mincer. Theodore Schultz was well into his work on the economics of education as well as continuing his influential work on economic growth. Arnold Harberger was making fundamental studies in public finance and developing a major role through both his work and his students in economic development.

My main work was to be in industrial organization. I already had Reuben Kessel and Lester Telser as colleagues, and to my great delight Ronald Coase joined us three years later. The main influence on me, however, was Aaron Director, with whom I had formed a close friendship at the first meeting of the Mt. Pelerin Society in 1946. Aaron was and is a paragon of all collegial virtues. He has a strong, independent mind and he has thought deeply on many questions, dissecting widely accepted and comfortable ideas to reveal their essential superficiality and frequent inconsistencies. He was in the law school, teaching primarily the antitrust course with Edward H. Levi, so his primary work was in antitrust economics.

I cannot recount the number of times in which Director's always courteous questioning led me either to change my views or to seek evidence to reinforce their relevance and weight. If we had been in Greece, I'm sure I would have called him Socrates. His questioning of McGee had already led to John's famous article on predatory pricing, his questioning of Telser soon contributed to Lester's famous article on resale price maintenance, and his questioning of Ward Bowman and Meyer Burstein and George Hilton led to their articles on price discrimination and the metering of demand. Concluding that Director would never write, later I was provoked to present one of his ideas with the title, "Director's Law of Income Redistribution."

A digression on research and originality

There is good reason for believing that economics is a social science in quite another sense from the indisputable one that it concerns itself with mankind in social relationships. It appears also to be a social science in the literal sense that it is a science in which it is difficult to do creative work if one is not in a congenial intellectual environment.

Consider the fact that two of the premier nations of Western Europe, France and Germany, have made on the whole rather minor contributions to the evolution of modern economic analysis. They are nations with long histories of preeminence in mathematics and with great periods in physics, chemistry, and astronomy. Therefore we cannot ascribe their minor roles in economics to lack of powerful scientific capacities. Nor can we easily believe that these nations were sufficiently different in their social or economic or political systems from that of Great Britain so that they should have less reason to be interested in political economy.

Consider again the fact that economics has been characterized by periods of intense scientific progress and controversy, periods that have often lasted for several generations. Cambridge University was the scene of such activity, almost without a break, from 1890 to 1940, and Vienna has a similar history beginning twenty years earlier and also ending in the thirties. Or consider Chicago, which has been the home of similarly intense activity in economics from the 1930s to the present. These periods of sustained scientific enterprise must have some elements of a chain reaction. Indeed, the very notion of a Cambridge or Austrian or Chicago school implies the existence of more than one gifted person with a temporary coterie of disciples.

I will be told, most properly, that von Thünen and Gossen or Cournot were hardly minor economic theorists, just to cite examples from the Germany and France that I have said made rather minor contributions to economics. They were theorists of great creativity, but, as I argued earlier, they did not have any influence upon their contemporaries. The main reason, at least in the case of the two Germans, must have been their intellectual isolation. That isolation allowed von Thünen to spend prodigious energies on the attempt to discover the formula for a God-given fair wage, a will-of-the-wisp that he asked to have engraved on his tombstone ($\sqrt{ap}$). Gossen's book gets its ferocious difficulty not from the inherent complexity of his analysis but from its cryptic, crabbed, unmotivated exposition. Able colleagues would have helped to harness these geniuses. Cournot's book was in one respect similar: despite its splendid lucidity, it was written in a language of mathematics that no important contemporary economist was prepared to speak.

If scientific work is a social activity, discovery is surely not. The discovery of a new theory or a new dimension of an existing theory is an act of creativity that is most imperfectly understood, at least by me. We have little understanding of why Jevons and Gossen discovered marginal utility theory, rather than John

Stuart Mill and Senior—certainly the latter two possessed the ingredients and the ability. I have given the explanation for the *adoption* of the utility theory by the profession that it only became useful as economics became a formalized study of academicians in the latter part of the nineteenth century.[1] Even if this is correct it does not explain how a young assayer in the mint in Sydney, Australia, or an unsuccessful minor civil servant in Germany came upon the idea.

Something can perhaps be said about the sources of new ideas in economics. I believe that we can usually divide new economic ideas into two classes: those that arise out of the critical examination of the ideas of other economists, and those that seek directly to explain some body of empirical phenomena. The classes are not sharply exclusive because the ideas of other economists are presumably directed ultimately to the explanation of real phenomena and therefore are a conduit to those phenomena. Nevertheless, the classification has some value, I believe.

Consider two greats of the late Victorian period, Walras and Marshall. Walras sought to construct a consistent theoretical structure to describe the nature of an enterprise economy. Almost nothing in that elegant structure was calculated to explain any observable behavior, except only the phenomenon of negatively sloping demand curves—and even that was not demonstrated.

Marshall, on the other hand, was concerned to explain the role of time in the formation of prices and the allocation of resources, and this is the central contribution of his *Principles*. He also made many improvements on predecessors' theories, a striking example being the identification of those elements of land (namely, its spatial relations and annuity of weather) that really constitute Ricardo's original and indestructible properties of the soil. Nevertheless, his eyes were mainly on economic phenomena to be explained, not on predecessors to be corrected.

It is worth pursuing Marshall's two kinds of work a step further. The influence of time was illustrated by a host of persuasive everyday examples, and this was proof enough to make market and short- and long-run normal prices a part of the standard theory of economics. The redefinition of land was elegant, for it isolated the proper empirical content of Ricardian land, but it had no effect upon subsequent economics. I attribute this, at least proximately, to Marshall's failure to show that this concept of land had interesting empirical or policy implications.

On my reckoning, the immediate stimulation to advances in economics has overwhelmingly been the attempt to improve on other economists' work. This was the primary source of stimulation for Ricardo, Mill, Edgeworth, Pigou, and most modern economists. Grappling directly with real phenomena is less popular, as well it might be, for the phenomena appear disorderly and poorly enumerated. Yet in addition to Marshall I would put much of the work of Smith, Keynes, and Friedman in this tradition.

For quite a few thousand years most new or unfamiliar ideas must have been wrong: if they were not, the task of being a well-educated scholar would be quite overwhelming. Many "new" ideas are not new at all, only unfamiliar, and most new or unfamiliar ideas are mistaken or infertile.

This raises the question of how a science adopts a new idea, which returns us to the social element in scientific work. Even the new ideas that are eventually judged by many to be good ideas are not often easily absorbed by a discipline. New ideas look at new things or look at familiar things in a new perspective, and their fertility and usefulness are not self-evident. They carry no label or halo that certifies their value, and the claims of their inventors are no different from the claims of the inventors of poor ideas.

A successful innovator therefore finds his work only half done when he has developed a new idea. Indeed the fraction is probably less than half, since the criticisms and misunderstandings his idea encounters will force him to work further on it. He will have to show how it can be developed further, how it is applicable in interesting ways, and how its weaknesses can be patched up. He will be much assisted in all this work if he can enlist a few fervent disciples. Not only may they help in developing the theory, but they can engage in a variety of controversies, which are the best of ways in which to publicize the idea.

If the discoverer lacks the energy or position to pursue the new idea, it is likely to lie fallow. A host of creative ideas—not only those of Cournot and Gossen but some of those of successful economists like Edgeworth and Pareto—required decades to become subjects of active investigation. In passing, I may remark that I have usually moved on to another subject fairly soon after working on one, and as I read the history of science that is a failing.

My work

Much the most important contribution I have made to economics is information theory. It could have originated in the attempt to generalize economic theories that usually assumed that economic actors had complete knowledge of their markets and technology. But it did not: my discomfort was with a theory that did not account for the fact that almost every product or service will have a distribution of prices, not a unique price, at a given time.

My own observations, partly of price data in antitrust areas, confirmed the existence of a variety of prices of a reasonably homogeneous good. The most obvious available explanation, product differentiation of Chamberlin's sort, seemed inappropriate to markets in automobiles of a given model at retail, bituminous coal, and the like. The apparent near-homogeneity of the products aside, there appeared to be no interesting empirical predictions derivable from monopolistic competition theory as to the extent of price dispersion, its changes over time, and the factors that led to the dispersion.

It occurred to me that it was the expensiveness of knowledge that sustained price differences. Search is never free and often expensive. To visit eight or ten automobile dealers in my search for a given automobile could cost a day plus transportation costs. To visit a second supermarket could require twenty minutes, and the average value of twenty minutes to an American adult is perhaps three dollars.

From the theory of search for the lowest price by a buyer or the highest price by a seller, we can deduce many corollaries. Clearly, the price dispersion relative to the average price will be less the more the buyer spends on it, because the costs of search do not go up as fast as the value of the commodity purchased. The dispersion of prices of automobiles relative to their average price will be lower than that of prices of microwave ovens. Again, knowledge decays gradually with the passage of time, so we expect goods bought frequently to have less price dispersion than infrequently purchased goods of equal value. The amount of search varies with the length of time one lives in a community, so tourists on average pay more for things than natives do.

I applied the theory to the labor markets and it shed light on a variety of the observed wage patterns. Information has other dimensions besides price, so I made a wholly different application of information to the problem of colluding oligopolists, where the central problem is to detect departures from the collusive agreement. Here I invoked observable quantities, not unobservable genuine transaction prices, to detect surreptitious competitive behavior. I also made an attempt to view the functions of advertising in this light, in contrast to the tradition of economists' hostility to advertising.

I must confess that I did not imagine the variety of informational problems in economics that would emerge in the next two decades. For a time it seemed essential to have the phrase "asymmetrical information" in the title of every journal article. Yet the subject is far from exhausted, and I have recently returned to the problem of political information.

I was not led to the economics of information by the previous literature; indeed that previous literature was virtually non-existent. Only later did I realize that a suggestive treatment resided in Charles Babbage's discussion of what he called the verification of prices.

My work in the theory of economic regulation has a different but related intellectual history. Starting in the early 1960s, I made a series of studies of the actual effects of several public regulatory policies: state utility commission regulation of electric utility rates; S.E.C. regulation of new stock issues; and the antitrust laws. I made these studies because I was skeptical of the prevailing practice in economics of treating the prescriptions of law as actual practice. My findings were often surprising: the regulation of electric utilities did not help residential users; the regulation of new stock issues did not help the widows and orphans who bought these issues.

Only slowly, I should say inexcusably slowly, did I come to the most obvious of questions: why do we get public regulation? I attempted to answer the question by looking at costs and benefits to the various parties. This approach was highly incompatible with the ruling approach in political science. There the introduction of a regulatory policy simply represented the response of the legislature to an aroused public demand for protection of the public interest. The demand of the public, in turn, was due to the existence and growth of some social evil, perhaps called to public attention by vigorous reformers. This "public interest" theory did very poorly in explaining protective tariffs or the farm program and had nothing to say about the dates at which policies were initiated: why was the social security system begun in the 1930s rather than the 1890s or the 1950s?

My work on regulation was much more closely related to that of others than was my work on information. Anthony Downs, James Buchanan, and Gordon Tullock had made large beginnings in the application of economic logic to politics, and my style of approach differed primarily in its strong empirical orientation.

These are examples of my theoretical work directed to the explanation of observed phenomena, with little or no relationship to the work of other economists. It is instructive to look also at a problem I worked on that emerged directly from the literature.

The determination of the efficient sizes of business enterprises is an interesting example. Economists sought to establish the most efficient size of enterprise in any industry by one of three methods: (1) a direct comparison of observed costs of enterprises of different sizes; (2) a direct comparison of rates of return on investment of enterprises of different sizes; and (3) an estimation of cost functions on the basis of technological information. Each of these methods encounters severe problems, always of data and often of logic.

I sought an answer by resorting to a sort of Darwinian approach, which had already been employed in a related manner by Alchian. My argument was essentially this: if I wish to know whether a tiger or a panther is the stronger animal, I put them in the same cage and return after a few hours. Similarly, by seeing the sizes to which firms competing in an industry were tending, I could deduce the efficient sizes—a method called the survivor technique.

The method seems obvious and, I later found, had antecedents as illustrious as John Stuart Mill, but for a considerable time the method encountered substantial opposition. The National

Bureau of Economic Research, where it was written, did not wish to publish it, perhaps because it was too controversial. There is no reliable way to discover something new: if there were, it would infallibly be discovered. It seems evident to me that Friedman's splendid theory of consumption function arose out of puzzles displayed by observable data, and Arrow's splendid impossibility theorem arose out of profound thought about the process of social decision making.

Conclusion

I should warn you, although I confess I should have done so at the outset rather than at the conclusion of this lecture, that I am a strong supporter of the view that a knowledge of the life of a scholar is more often a source of misunderstanding than of enlightenment about his work. Obviously, my arguments for this view have not been convincing, or Professor Breit would not have organized this lecture series.

The reason that this biographical approach—it bears the oppressive name of prosopography—is misleading is that its devotees usually pick out of a scholar's life some circumstance or event that they find explains a given theory. To give you real and absurd examples, one historian said life on a small island led Malthus to fear overpopulation; another said John Stuart Mill could not be original because he wrote his *Principles* in less that two years.

I am not prepared to say that one's work is independent of one's life. Possibly if I had gone to Harvard instead of Chicago, I would have been a believer in monopolistic competition, a student of input-output tables, or a member of the Mason school of industrial organization. But I do not attach high probabilities to these possibilities. I am no longer a faithful follower, although I am still an admirer, of Frank Knight and Henry Simons: each person has a mind-style of his own, and eventually it asserts itself. This does not mean that we are immune to our environment, but it does argue for me that environmental influences will be subtle.

I not only believe this to be true but also I hope that it is true: the prospects for scientific progress would be bleak if we could train our students to become truly faithful disciples. If you understand my scientific work better for having heard me, I shall be both pleased and envious.

Date of Birth

January 17, 1911

Academic Degrees

B.B.A. University of Washington, 1931

M.B.A. Northwestern University, 1932

Ph.D. University of Chicago, 1938

Academic Affiliations

Assistant Professor, Iowa State, 1936–1938

Assistant, Associate, and Full Professor, University of Minnesota, 1938–1946

Professor, Brown University, 1946–47

Professor, Columbia University, 1947–1958

Charles R. Walgreen Distinguished Service Professor of American Institutions, University of Chicago, 1958–1981

Director, Center for the Study of the Economy and the State, University of Chicago, 1977–present

Selected Books

The Citizen and the State: Essays on Regulation
Essays in the History of Economics
The Organization of Industry
Production and Distribution Theories
The Theory of Price

James Tobin

Beginning with Keynes at Harvard

Rare is the child, I suspect, who wants to grow up to be an economist, or a professor. I grew up in a university town and went to a university-run high school, where most of my friends were faculty kids. I was so unfailing an A student that it was boring even to me. But I don't recall thinking of an academic career. I liked journalism, my father's occupation; I had put out "newspapers" of my own from age six. I thought of law; I loved to argue, and beginning in my teens I was fascinated by politics. I guess I knew that there was economics at the university, but I didn't know what the subject really was. Of course, economic issues were always coming up in classes on history and government—civics, in those days. I expected economics to be among the social science courses I would someday take in college, probably part of the pre-law curriculum.

I grew up happily assuming I would go to college in my hometown, to the University of Illinois. One month before I was scheduled to enroll as a freshman, I was offered and accepted a Conant Prize Fellowship at Harvard. I should explain how this happened. My father, a learned man, a voracious reader, the biggest customer of the Champaign Public Library, discovered in the *New York Times* that Harvard was offering two of these new fellowships in each of five midwestern states. President Conant wanted to broaden the geographical and social base of Harvard College. Having nothing to lose, I accepted my father's suggestion that I apply. University High School, it turned out, had without even trying prepared me superbly for the obligatory College Board exams. Uni High graduates only thirty to thirty-five persons a year, but it has three Nobels to its credit and, once I had broken the ice, many national scholarships.

Thus James Bryant Conant, Louis Michael Tobin, and University High School changed my life and career. Illinois was and is a great university. But I doubt that it would have led me into economics. For several reasons, Harvard did.

Harvard was the leading academic center of economics in North America at the time; only Columbia and Chicago were close competitors. Both its senior and junior faculty were outstanding. Two of the previous lecturers in this series were active and influential members of the community when I was a student, Wassily Leontief on the faculty and Paul Samuelson as a Junior Fellow, a graduate student free of formal academic requirements. Of the senior faculty of the 1930s, Joseph Schumpeter would have been a sure bet for a Nobel, Alvin Hansen, Edward Chamberlin, and Gottfried Haberler likely choices. Haberler, still active, remains a possibility. Naturally, Harvard attracted remarkably talented graduate students. That able undergraduates might go on to scholarly careers was taken for granted.

When I arrived at Harvard, I knew I would want to major—at Harvard the word is *concentrate*—in one of the social sciences or possibly in mathematics. By the end of freshman year I was leaning to economics. But I hadn't yet taken any. In those days even Ec A, the introductory course, was considered too hard for freshmen. As a sophomore all of eighteen years old, I began Ec A in a section taught by Spencer Pollard, an advanced graduate student specializing in labor economics and writing a dissertation on John L. Lewis and the United Mine Workers.

Pollard was also my tutor. A Harvard undergraduate, besides taking four courses, met regularly, usually singly, with a tutor in his field of concentration, generally a faculty member or graduate student associated with the student's residential house. Tutorial was not graded. It was modeled, like the house system itself, on Oxford and Cambridge. Pollard suggested that we devote our sessions to "this new book from England." He had recently been over there and judged from the stir the book was creating even before publication that it was important. The book was *The General Theory of Employment, Interest and Money* by John Maynard Keynes, published in 1936.

Pollard was no respecter of academic conventions; that I was only an Ec A student meant nothing to him. I was too young, and too ready to assume that teacher knows best, to know that I knew too little to read the book. So I read it, and Pollard and I talked about it as we went through it. Cutting my teeth on *The General Theory*, I was hooked on economics.

Like many other economists of my vintage, I was attracted to the field for two reasons. One was that economic theory is a fascinating intellectual challenge, on the order of mathematics or chess. I liked analytics and logical argument. I thought algebra was the most eye-opening school experience between the three Rs and college.

The other reason was the obvious relevance of economics to understanding and perhaps overcoming the great depression and all the frightening political developments associated with it throughout the world. I did not personally suffer deprivations during the depression. But my parents made me very conscious of the political and economic problems of the times. My father was a well-informed and thoughtful political liberal. My mother was a social worker, recalled to her career by the emergency; she was dealing with cases of unemployment and poverty every day.

The second motivation, I observe, gave our generation of economists different interests and priorities from subsequent cohorts dominated by those attracted to the subject more exclusively by the appeal of its puzzles to their quantitative aptitudes and interests.

Thanks to Keynes, economics offered me the best of both worlds. I was fascinated by his theoretical duel with the orthodox classical economists. Keynes's uprising against encrusted error was an appealing crusade for youth. The truth would make us free, and fully employed too. I was already an ardent and uncritical New Dealer, much concerned about the depression, unemployment, and poverty. According to Keynesian theory, Roosevelt's devaluation of the dollar and deficit spending were sound economics after all.

By sheer application, unconstrained by the need to unlearn anything, I came to know Keynes's new book sooner and better than many of my elders at Harvard. Keynes was the founder of what later came to be known as macroeconomics, what his young associate Joan Robinson called at the time "the theory of output as a whole," a phrase I found strikingly apt. The contrast was with the theory of output and price in particular markets or sectors. This—what we now call "micro"—was the main stuff of the theory course we economics concentrators took after Ec A. I liked the methodology of the new subject, modeling the whole economy by a system of simultaneous equations; by now I had calculus to add to my algebra. J. R. Hicks and others showed, more clearly than Keynes himself, how the essentials of *The General Theory*, and its differences from classical theory, could be expressed and analyzed in such models.

Harvard was becoming the beachhead for the Keynesian invasion of the new world. The senior faculty was mostly hostile. A group of them had not long before published a book quite critical of Roosevelt's recovery program. Seymour Harris, an early convert to Keynes, was an exception, especially important to undergraduates like myself, in whom he took a paternal interest. Harris was an academic entrepreneur. He opened the pages of the *Review of Economics and Statistics*, of which he was editor, and the halls of Dunster House, of which he was senior tutor, to lively debates on economic theory and policy. The younger faculty and the graduate student teaching fellows were enthusiastic about Keynes's book. Their reasons were similar to my own but better informed. A popular tract by seven of them, *An Economic Program for American Democracy*, preached the new gospel with a left-wing slant.

Most important of all was the arrival of Alvin Hansen to fill the new Littauer chair in political economy. Hansen, aged fifty, came to Harvard from the University of Minnesota the same year I was beginning economics. He had previously been critical of Keynes and had indeed published a lukewarm review of *The General Theory*. He changed his mind 180 degrees, a rare event for scholars of any age, especially if their previous views are in print. Hansen became the leading apostle of Keynesian theory and policy in America. His fiscal policy seminar was the focus of research, theoretical and applied, in Keynesian economics. Visitors from the Washington firing lines mixed with local students and faculty; I had the feeling that history was being made in that room. For undergraduates the immediate payoff was that Hansen taught us macroeconomics, though under the course rubric Money and Banking. Hansen was a true hero to me, and in later years he was to be a real friend also.

I wrote my senior honors thesis on what I perceived to be the central theoretical issue between Keynes and the classical economists he was attacking. The orthodox position was that prices move to clear markets, rising to eliminate excesses of demand over supply and falling to eliminate excess supplies. Applied to the labor market, this meant that reductions of wages would get rid of unemployment. Excess supply of labor could not be a permanent equilibrium. Unless wage cuts are prevented by law or by monopolistic trade unions, competition for jobs will lower wages and in turn restore or create jobs for the unemployed. This was just an application of the central thesis of orthodox economics, the Invisible Hand proposition of Adam Smith. Individual agents are selfish and myopic. They respond in their own interest to the market signals locally available to them. Their actions miraculously turn out for the best for the society as a whole. Competition brings this miracle about.

Keynes's heresy was to deny that this mechanism could be counted on to eliminate involuntary unemployment. He didn't say just that the mechanism was slow and needed help from government policy. He said it might not work at all. Instead, the economy would be stuck in an underemployment equilibrium. Orthodox economists thought they could prove that free competitive markets allocate resources efficiently. In saying that willing and productive workers can't get jobs, Keynes was indicting the market system for a massive failure. After all, there is no greater inefficiency than to leave productive resources idle.

My honors thesis found fault with Keynes's logic. That may seem surprising. But I didn't think Keynes needed to insist on so sweeping a theoretical victory on his opponents' home court. His practical message was just as important whether unemployment was an incident of prolonged disequilibrium or of equilibrium. My first professional publication (1941) was an article in the *Quarterly Journal of Economics* based on my senior thesis; the *QJE* is, of course, edited and published at Harvard. The issue is very much alive today. It has also remained an interest of mine, a subject on which I have published several other papers, including my 1971 presidential address to the American Economic Association (1972).

Tools of the trade, theoretical and statistical

By graduation time in 1939 I had forgotten about law and drifted into the natural decision, to become a professional economist. Harvard has a way of keeping its own: my fellowship was extended and I went on to graduate school. The transition was easy; I had taken courses with graduate students while I was a senior. Now I needed to pick up some tools of the trade. One was formal mathematical economic theory, and another was statistics and econometrics. Harvard was just beginning to catch up to the state of these two arts.

I see in retrospect that our professors left most of our education to us. They expected us to teach ourselves and learn from each other, and we did. They treated us as adult partners in scholarly endeavor, not as apprentices. I am afraid our graduate programs today try too hard to convey a definite and vast body of material and to test how well students master what we know. I wrote my undergraduate thesis under the nominal supervision of my senior-year tutor, Professor Edward Chamberlin. He said he knew nothing about my subject and left me on my own. Our tutorial sessions were nonetheless interesting; we argued about Catholic agrarianism, his vision of economic utopia. The faculty adviser for my doctoral dissertation in 1946–47 was, by my choice, Professor Schumpeter, one of the truly great economists, indeed social scientists, of the century. He had no use for Keynes and little for my topic, the consumption function. He read what I wrote and made helpful suggestions, but mostly he kept hands off. When I saw him, we talked of many other things, to my lasting benefit.

The theory we were taught was largely in the Anglo-American tradition, in which mathematical argument was subordinated to verbal and graphical exposition and relegated to footnotes. The great book was *Principles of Economics* by Alfred Marshall, Keynes's own mentor in the other Cambridge. Markets were analyzed mostly one at a time—*partial* equilibrium analysis. Little rigorous attempt was made to describe a *general* equilibrium of the system as a whole, with many commodities, many consumers and producers, many markets interconnected with each other.

Mathematical models of general equilibrium were a stronger tradition in continental Europe, to which the French-Swiss economist Leon Walras had made the seminal contribution in 1870. Though F. Y. Edgeworth at Oxford and Irving Fisher at Yale had written in the same vein, they had not greatly influenced the main line of English-language economics from Adam Smith to David Ricardo to John Stuart Mill to Marshall. But in the late 1930s and 1940s the mathematical general equilibrium approach was coming into vogue, thanks to J. R. Hicks and R. G. D. Allen in Britain and Wassily Leontief and Paul Samuelson at Harvard. Joseph Schumpeter fostered this development, believing that Walras had provided economics its "magna charta," even though his own theory of the dynamics of capitalism was wholly different.

I liked the general equilibrium approach; that was one of the great appeals of macroeconomics. But those models of output as a whole were small enough and specific enough to understand and manipulate. I have never been an aficionado of formal mathematical general equilibrium theory, which is so pure and general as to be virtually devoid of interesting operational conclusions. Moreover, I have come to think that its elegance gives many economic theorists today an exaggerated presumptive faith that free competitive markets work for the best. I did use the approach in some articles in the late 1940s on the theory of rationing, all but one of them in collaboration with Hendrik Houthakker.

In statistics and econometrics Harvard was further behind the times. The professors who taught economic statistics were idiosyncratic in the methods they used and quite suspicious of methods based in mathematical statistical theory. Until the 1950s Harvard was pretty much untouched by the developments in Europe led by Ragnar Frisch and Jan Tinbergen or those in the United States at the Cowles Commission. Students like me, who were interested in formal statistical theory, took refuge in the mathematics department. For econometrics we squeezed as much as possible from a seminar on statistical demand functions offered by a European visitor, Hans Staehle. We also discovered that regressions, though scorned by professors Crum and Frickey, were alive and well under the aegis of Professor John D. Black's program in agricultural economics. In the basement of Littauer Center we could use his electromechanical or manual Marchands and Monroes.

I did just that for my second published paper (1942), originally written for Edward S. Mason's seminar in spring semester 1941, on how to use statistical forecasts in defense planning; my example was estimation of civilian demands for steel. The paper was one reason Mason recommended me for a job in Washington with the civilian supply division of the nascent Office of Price Administration and Civilian Supply. So I left Harvard in May 1941, having completed all the requirements for the Ph.D. except the dissertation. I would not return until February 1946. After nine months of helping to ration scarce materials, I went in the Navy and served as a line officer on a destroyer until Christmas 1945.

Statistics and econometrics were important in my research after the war. In my doctoral dissertation (1947) on the determinants of household consumption and saving, I tried to marry "cross-section" data from family budget surveys with aggregate time series, the better to estimate effects of income, wealth, and other variables. In a later study of food demand (1950), I refined the method. This, along with my empirical and theoretical work on rationing, took place in England in 1949–50, at Richard Stone's Department of Applied Economics in Cambridge. I hoped that cross-section observations could resolve the ambiguities of statistical inference based on time series alone. Later my interest in cross-section and panel data led me to the work of the Michigan Survey Research Center, where I spent a fruitful semester with George Katona, James Morgan, and Lawrence Klein in 1953.

My work on data of this type led me to propose a new statistical method, which became known as Tobit analysis (1958). Probit analysis, which originated in biology, estimates how the probabilities of positive or negative responses to treatment depend on observed characteristics of the organism and the treatment. In economic applications, Yes responses often vary in intensity; for example, most families in a sample would report No when asked if they bought a car last year, while those who answer Yes spent varying amounts of money on a car. My technique would use both Yes-No and quantitative information in seeking the determinants of car purchases.

The label Tobit was perhaps more appropriate than Arthur Goldberger thought when he introduced it in his textbook. Perhaps not. My main claim to fame, a discovery enjoyed by generations of my students, is that, thinly disguised as a midshipman named Tobit, I make a fleeting appearance in Herman Wouk's novel *The Caine Mutiny*. Wouk and I attended the same quick Naval Reserve officers' training school at Columbia in spring 1942, and so did Willy, the hero of the novel.

Innovative and seminal work in mathematical economics and econometrics took place at the Cowles Commission for Research in Economics in the years 1944–1954. The commission was then affiliated with the University of Chicago. Its research output over that period is one of the most fruitful achievements in the history of organized scientific inquiry. The leaders were Jacob Marschak and Tjalling Koopmans; Koopmans was awarded a Nobel Prize for his contributions to the theory of resource allocation, including linear programming, during this period. The remarkable teams Marschak and Koopmans assembled included two of the previous speakers in this series at Trinity, Arrow and Klein, and two other Nobel laureates, Simon and Debreu. When I was a graduate student at Harvard after the war, I stood in awe of the Cowles Commission and of Marschak and Koopmans. I came to know them at meetings of the Econometric Society. For the December 1947 meeting in Chicago I was asked to be a discussant of a paper by Marschak. I didn't get the paper until a few days before the meeting, indeed a day or so before Christmas. I worked hard on the paper—neglecting my wife, Betty, pregnant with our first child, and holiday festivities with our families. I was able to report some important flaws in Marschak's model and to offer some constructive suggestions. One thing led to another. I was asked to join the commission, and in 1954 I was asked to become its research director, to succeed Koopmans as he had succeeded Marschak.

The offer was flattering, challenging, and tempting. But I was very happy at Yale, and Betty and I had come to like New Haven very much as a place to live and raise a family. It turned out that we could have our cake and eat it too. Koopmans was quite interested in relocating the commission, because of difficulties in attracting staff to Chicago at that time and problems in the relation between the commission and the university. He gave me not the slightest inkling of this interest until I had definitely declined the offer. The founder and financial angel of the commission, Alfred Cowles, was a Yale graduate; he hoped his creation could find permanent hospitality from his alma mater.

In 1955 the commission moved to Yale, renamed the Cowles Foundation for Research in Economics at Yale University. I became its research director after all. Cowles Foundation Discussion Paper 1 (1955) was a precursor of the Tobit analysis mentioned above. The coming of Cowles was an important factor in the rise of economics at Yale to front-rank stature.

I broadened the scope of the foundation's research to include macroeconomics. I was particularly eager to make room for the interests and talents of a young Yale assistant professor, Arthur Okun, who was working on macroeconomic forecasting and policy analysis.

Developing Keynesian macroeconomics; synthesizing it with the neoclassical tradition

My main program of research and writing after the war continued my early interests in Keynes and macroeconomics. I sought to improve the theoretical foundations of macro models, to fit them into the main corpus of neoclassical economics, and to clarify the roles of monetary and fiscal policies. In this endeavor I shared the objectives of many other economists, notably Abba Lerner, Paul Samuelson, Franco Modigliani, Robert Solow, J. R. Hicks, and James Meade. A new mainstream, synthesizing the Keynesian revolution and the classical economics against which it was revolting, was in the making. I am proud that Paul Samuelson called me a "partner in [this] crime."

The building blocks of the Keynesian structure were four in number: the relation of wages and employment; the propensity to consume; liquidity preference and the demand for money; the inducement to invest. I have already referred to my work on the first. I turn now to the other three.

Keynes's "psychological law" of consumption and saving stated that saving would be an ever-larger proportion of income as per capita real incomes became greater. National income data between the two world wars appeared to confirm his law. Statistical equations, fit to those data, extrapolated to much higher incomes, foretold trouble after the Second World War. Investment would have to be a much larger fraction of national income than ever before to absorb the high saving and avoid recession and unemployment. The extrapolation was wrong.

Incomes rose as expected, but consumption was no smaller a proportion than before. This forecasting error triggered an agonizing reappraisal of the consumption function, with fruitful results. My doctoral dissertation (1947) was on this subject. I thought Keynes's law should be interpreted to refer to the relation of lifetime consumption to lifetime income, not to a relation between those variables year by year. The same considerations implied that wealth, not just current income, determines consumption in the short run. As so often happens, this idea was in the air. Milton Friedman's permanent income theory and Franco Modigliani's life-cycle model were elegant explanations of saving behavior in this spirit. They showed how cyclical data could look "Keynesian" even though saving would be roughly proportional to income in the long run. I have written a number of papers on this subject over the years.

The episode is, I believe, an example of how economic knowledge advances, when striking real-world events and issues pose puzzles we have to try to understand and resolve. The most important decisions a scholar makes are what problems to work on. Choosing them just by looking for gaps in the literature is often not very productive and at worst divorces the literature itself from problems that provide more important and productive lines of inquiry. The best economists have taken their subjects from the world around them.

The bulk of my work in the 1950s and 1960s was on the monetary side of macroeconomics. I had several objectives.

First, I wanted to establish a firm foundation for the sensitivity of money demand or money velocity to interest rates. Why was this important? The quantity theory of money, later called monetarism, asserted that there was no such sensitivity, that the velocity of money was constant except for random shocks and for slow, secular changes in public habits, banking institutions, and financial technology. The implication was that fiscal stimulus, such as government spending or tax reduction, could not affect aggregate spending on goods and services unless accompanied by money creation. The same implication applied to autonomous changes in private investment. In this sense Milton Friedman and other monetarists were saying not just that money matters, with which I agreed, but also that money is all that matters, with which I disagreed.

In an empirical paper in 1947 I let the data speak for themselves, loudly in favor of Keynes's liquidity preference curve. But I was not satisfied with Keynes's explanation of liquidity preference. He said people preferred liquid cash because they expected interest rates to rise to "normal" prosperity levels of the past, causing capital losses on holdings of bonds. As William Fellner, later to be my colleague at Yale, pointed out in a friendly debate with me in journal pages, Keynes could hardly call "equilibrium" a situation in which interest rates are persistently lower than investors' expectations of them. Fellner was espousing a principle of model building later called "rational expectations," and I agreed with him.

I found and offered two more tenable sources of the interest sensitivity of demand for money. One (1956) was based on an inventory theory of the management of transactions balances. As I learned too late, I had been mostly anticipated by William Baumol, but the model is commonly cited with both names. The second paper (1958) gave a new rationalization of Keynes's "speculative motive": simply, aversion to risk. People may prefer liquidity, and prefer it more the lower the interest rate on noncash assets, not because they expect capital losses on average but because they fear them more than they value the equally probable capital gains.

I had been working for some time on portfolio choices balancing such risks against expected returns, and the liquidity preference paper was an exposition and application of that work. Harry Markowitz had already set forth a similar model of portfolio choice, and our paths also converged geographically when he spent a year at Yale in 1955–56. My interest was in macroeconomic implications, his more in advising rational investors.

When my prize was announced in Stockholm in 1981, the first reports that reached this country mentioned portfolio theory. This caught the interest of the reporters who faced me at a hastily arranged press conference at Yale. They wanted to know what it was, so I did my best to explain it in lay language, after which they said "Oh no, please explain it in lay language." That's when I referred to the benefits of diversification: "You know, don't put all your eggs in one basket." And that is why headlines throughout the world said "Yale economist wins Nobel for 'Don't put all your eggs. . . ,' " and why a friend of mine sent me a cartoon he had clipped, which followed that headline with a sketch of next year's winner in medicine explaining how his award was for "An apple a day keeps the doctor away."

The fact that one of the available assets in the model of my paper was riskless turned out to have interesting consequences. I felt somewhat uneasy and apologetic that I was pairing the safe asset with just one risky asset to represent everything else. This aggregation followed Keynes, who also used "*the* interest rate" to refer to the common yield on all nonmoney assets and debts. I proved that my results would apply even if any number of risky assets were available, each with different return and risk. The choice of a risky portfolio, the relative weights of the various risky assets within it, would be independent of the decision how much to put into risky assets relative to the safe asset, money. This "separation theorem" was the key to the capital asset pricing model developed by Lintner and Sharpe, beloved by finance teachers and students, and exploited by the investment managers and counselors who compute and report the "betas" of various securities.

The debate about fiscal and monetary policy, as related to the interest-sensitivity of demand for money, went on for a long time, too much of it a duel between Milton Friedman and me. In a Vermont ski line a young attendant checking season passes read mine and said in a French-Canadian accent, "Tobeen, James Tobeen, not ze economiste! Not ze enemy of Professeur Friedman!" He was an economics student in Quebec; it made his day. He let me pass to the lift. This debate, I would say, ended for practical purposes when Friedman shifted ground, saying that no important issue of monetary policy or theory depended on interest-sensitivity of money demand. The ground he shifted to was the basic issue between Keynes and the classics, the contention that the economy is always in a supply-constrained equilibrium where neither monetary nor fiscal policy can enhance real output.

Second, I proposed to put money into the theory of long-run growth. In the 1950s one phase of the synthesis of Keynesian and neoclassical economics was the development of a growth theory along neoclassical lines. Some, not all, Keynesians were ready to agree that in the long run employment is full, saving limits investment, and "supply creates its own demand." The short run was the Keynesian domain, where labor and capital may be underemployed, investment governs saving, and demand induces its own supply. Roy Harrod had started modern growth theory in 1939, followed by Evsey Domar in the 1940s and Trevor Swan, Robert Solow, Edmund Phelps, and many others in the 1950s and 1960s.

I was involved too. My 1955 piece, "A Dynamic Aggregative Model," may be my favorite; it was the most fun to write. It differed from the other growth literature by explicitly introducing monetary government debt as a store of value, a vehicle of saving alternative to real capital, and by generating a business cycle that interrupted the growth process. In three subsequent papers (1965, 1968, and 1985) I showed that the stock of capital in a growing economy is positively related to the rates of monetary growth and inflation.

Third, in a long series of papers I developed, together with William Brainard and other colleagues at Yale, a general model of asset markets and integrated it into a full macroeconomic model. In a sense we generalized Hicks's famous IS/LM formalization of Keynes by allowing for a richer menu of assets. As I already indicated, I had been uncomfortable with that unique "*the* interest rate" in Keynes and with the simple dichotomy of money versus everything else, usually described as money versus bonds. I thought nominal assets versus real capital was at least as important a way of splitting wealth, if it must be split in only two parts, and this is what I did in the growth models cited above.

Portfolio theory suggested that assets should be regarded as imperfect substitutes for each other, with their differences in expected yields reflecting their marginal risks. Our approach also suggested that there is no sharp dividing line between assets that are money and those that are not. The "Yale approach" to monetary and financial theory has been widely used in empirical flow-of-funds studies and in modeling international capital movements.

Our approach also explicitly recognizes the stock-flow dynamics of saving, investment, and asset accumulation, as in my 1981 Nobel lecture. These dynamics were explicitly ignored in Keynes, who defined the short run as a period in which the change in the stock of capital due to the flow of new investment is insignificant. Stock-flow dynamics are also ignored in IS/LM models. But flows do add to stocks. Investment builds the capital stock, government deficits enlarge the stocks of government bonds and possibly of money, trade surpluses increase the net assets of the nation vis-à-vis the rest of the world, and so on. Without these effects, macro stories about policies and other events are incomplete.

The bottom line of monetary policy is its effect on capital investment, in business plant and equipment, residences, inventories, and consumer durable goods. The effect is not well represented by the market interest rates usually cited, or by quantities of money or credit. Our approach to monetary economics and macroeconomics led us naturally to a different measure, closer to investment decisions. This has become known as "Tobin's q." It is the ratio of the market valuations of capital assets to their replacement costs, for example, the prices of existing houses relative to the costs of building comparable new ones. For corporate businesses, the market valuations are made in the securities markets. It is common sense that the incentive to make new capital investments is high when the securities giving title to their future earnings can be sold for more than the investments cost, i.e., when q exceeds one. We see the reverse in takeovers of companies whose qs are less than one; it is cheaper to buy their productive assets by acquiring their shares than to construct comparable facilities from scratch. That is why in our models q is the link from the central bank and the financial markets to the real economy.

Policy and public service

As must be clear from my narrative, I have always been intensely interested in economic policy. Much of my theoretical and empirical research has been devoted to analyzing and discerning the effects of monetary and fiscal policies. In the 1950s I began writing occasional articles on current economic issues for general readership, some of them in *The New Republic*, *The Yale Review*, *Challenge*, the *New York Times*.

Some of my friends in Massachusetts were advising Senator Kennedy. They told him and his staff about me. In summer 1960 Ted Sorenson came to see me and arranged for the Kennedy campaign to employ me to write some memoranda and position papers on economic growth. Sorenson signed me up despite the fact that I had felt it necessary to tell him I favored Stevenson for the nomination. I didn't notice any effects of my memos during the campaign, but I was told that they were used by the Kennedy team at the party platform deliberations, mainly to oppose the exaggerated "spend to grow" views of Leon Keyserling and some union economists.

My message at the time was that we needed a tight budget, one that would yield a surplus at full employment, and a very easy monetary policy, one that would get interest rates low enough to channel the government's surplus into productive capital investment. The point was to have full employment, but by a mix of policies that promoted growth in the economy's capacity to produce. Incidentally, my message is similar today.

After the 1960 election I served on a transition task force on the domestic economy chaired by Paul Samuelson. One day in early January 1961 I was summoned from lunch at the faculty club to take a phone call from the president-elect. He asked me to serve as a member of his Council of Economic Advisers. JT: "I'm afraid you've got the wrong guy, Mr. President. I'm an ivory-tower economist." JFK: "That's the best kind. I'll be an ivory-tower president." JT: "That's the best kind." I took a day or two to talk to Betty and to my colleagues and then said Yes. I served for twenty months.

Walter Heller was the chairman of the council, and Kermit Gordon was the other member. We had a fantastic staff, including Art Okun, Bob Solow, Ken Arrow, and a younger generation whose names would also be recognized as leaders in our profession today. We were all congenial, intellectually and personally, and we functioned by consensus without hierarchy or bureaucracy. We were optimistic, confident that our economics could improve policy and do good in the world. It was the opportunity that had motivated me to embrace economics a quarter century before.

The January 1962 *Economic Report* is the manifesto of our economics, applied to the United States and world economic conditions of the day. The press called it "the new economics," but it was essentially the blend of Keynesian and neoclassical economics we had been developing and elaborating for the previous ten years. The report was a collective effort, written mainly by Heller, Gordon, Solow, Okun, and Tobin. It doesn't appear on my personal bibliography, but I am proud of it as a work of professional economics as well as a public document. The January 1982 *Report* is the comparable document of Reaganomics, likewise the effort of professional economists to articulate a radically new approach to federal economic policy. It is interesting to compare the two; we have nothing to fear.

The Kennedy council was effective and influential because the president and his immediate White House staff took academics seriously, took ideas seriously, took us seriously. JFK was innocent of economics on inauguration day. But he was an interested, curious, keen, and able student. He read what we wrote, listened to what we said, and learned a lot.

Our central macroeconomic objective was to lower unemployment, 7 percent in January 1961, to 4 percent, our tentative estimate of the inflation-safe unemployment rate. That goal was achieved by the end of 1965, with negligible increase in the rate of inflation and with a big increase in capital investment. The sweet success turned sour in the late 1960s, when contrary to the advice of his council and other Keynesian advisers President Johnson failed to raise taxes to pay for the escalating costs of the war in Vietnam. Critics looking back on the 1960s accuse the Kennedy-Johnson economists of naïve belief in a Phillips trade-off and of policies explicitly designed to purchase lower unemployment with higher inflation. The criticism is not justified. The council did not propose to push unemployment below what came to be known as the "natural rate." Moreover, beginning in 1961 the council and the administration adopted wage and price policies designed to achieve an inflation-free recovery—"guideposts for noninflationary price and wage behavior" were espoused in the report.

I returned to Yale in September 1962. I loved the job at the council, but I knew my principal vocation was university teaching and research. Fifteen-hour days and seven-day weeks were a hardship for me, my wife, and our four young children. I remained active as a consultant to the council, particularly on international monetary issues that had concerned me as a member. Moreover, I was now more visible outside my profession, so I wrote and spoke more frequently on issues and controversies of the day. But I knew that alumni of Washington often have difficulty getting back into mainline professional scholarship. I determined to accomplish that re-entry, and I believe I did.

Kennedy and Johnson added the war on poverty to their agenda. Walter Heller and the council were very much involved. I became quite interested in the economic disadvantages of blacks and in the inadequacies, inefficiencies, and perverse incentives—penalties for work and marriage—of federal and state welfare programs. I wrote major papers on these matters in 1965 and 1968. This was not macroeconomics, but one implication of the Keynesian-neoclassical synthesis was that welfare and redistributional policies could be, within broad limits, chosen independently of macroeconomic goals. Nothing in our view of the functioning of capitalist democracies says either that prosperity requires hard-hearted welfare policies and small governments or that it requires redistribution in favor of workers and the poor.

I favored a negative income tax. So did Milton Friedman—although his version seemed to me too small to fill much of the poverty gap, and he refused to join a national nonpartisan statement of economists favoring the approach. I helped to design a negative income tax plan for George McGovern in 1972. Unfortunately, he and his staff botched its presentation in the heat of the California primary; I am sure most people to this day think McGovern was advocating a kooky budget-breaking handout. After the election Nixon proposed a family assistance plan pretty much the same as the McGovern scheme he had ridiculed during the campaign.

I have lived long enough to see the revolution to which I was an eager recruit fifty years ago become in its turn a mainstream orthodoxy and then the target of counterrevolutionary attack. The tides of political opinion and professional fashion have turned against me. Many of my young colleagues in the profession are as enthusiastic exponents of the new classical macroeconomics as I and my contemporaries were crusaders against old classical macroeconomics in the 1930s. Many of the issues are the same, but the environment is quite different from the great depression. The contesting factions are better equipped—our profession has certainly improved its mathematical, analytical, and statistical tools. I do not despair over the present divisions of opinion in economics. Our subject has always thrived and advanced through controversy, and I expect a new synthesis will evolve, maybe even in my lifetime. I haven't abandoned the field of battle myself. I hope I learn from the new, but I still think and say that Keynesian ideas about how the economy works and what policies can make it work better are relevant today—not just as Keynes wrote them, of course, but as they have been modified, developed, and refined over the last half-century.

Date of Birth

March 5, 1918

Academic Degrees

A.B.   Harvard University, 1939
M.A.   Harvard University, 1940
Ph.D. Harvard University, 1947

Academic Affiliations

Junior Fellow, Harvard University, 1946–1950
Associate Professor of Economics, Yale University, 1950–1955
Professor of Economics, Yale University, 1955–1957
Sterling Professor of Economics, Yale University, 1957–present

Selected Books

The American Business Creed (with S. E. Harris et al.)
National Economic Policy
Essays in Economics: Macroeconomics
The New Economics One Decade Older
Essays in Econometrics: Consumption and Econometrics

Notes

Introduction

1. For an authoritative discussion of the history, purpose, and qualifications for the Nobel Prize in Economics by one of the members of the Prize Committee, see Assar Lindbeck, "The Prize in Economic Science in Memory of Alfred Nobel," *Journal of Economic Literature* 23 (March 1985): 37–56.

Klein

1. *The Brookings Quarterly Econometric Model of the United States*, eds. J. Duesenberry, G. Fromm, L. Klein, and E. Kuh (Chicago: Rand McNally, 1965); *The Brookings Model: Some Further Results*, eds. J. Duesenberry, G. Fromm, L. Klein, and E. Kuh (Chicago: Rand McNally, 1969); *The Brookings Model: Perspectives and Recent Developments*, eds. G. Fromm and L. Klein (Amsterdam: North-Holland, 1975).

2. Irma and Frank Adelman, "The Dynamic Properties of the Klein-Goldberger Model," *Econometrica* 27 (October 1959): 596–625; H. Wagner, "A Monte Carlo Study of Estimates of Simultaneous Linear Structural Equations," *Econometrica* 26 (January 1958): 117–133.

3. The evolution of project LINK is spelled out in three volumes and updated by some descriptive articles. See R. J. Ball, *The International Linkage of National Economic Models*, J. Waelbroeck, *The Models of Project LINK*, J. Sawyer, *Modelling the International Transmission Mechanism* (Amsterdam: North-Holland, 1973, 1976, 1979); B. G. Hickman and L. R. Klein, "A Decade of Research by Project LINK," *ITEMS*, Social Science Research Council, N.Y. (December 1979); 49–56; L. R. Klein, Peter Pauly, and Pascal Voisin, "The World Economy—A Global Model," *Perspectives in Computing* 2 (May 1982): 4–17.

Stigler

1. "The Adoption of the Marginal Utility Theory," reprinted in G. J. Stigler, *The Economist as Preacher* (Chicago: University of Chicago Press, 1982): 72–85.